AIR VANGUARD 20

LOCKHEED SR-71 BLACKBIRD

PAUL F. CRICKMORE

First published in Great Britain in 2015 by Osprey Publishing,
PO Box 883, Oxford, OX1 9PL, UK
PO Box 3985, New York, NY 10185-3985, USA
E-mail: info@ospreypublishing.com

Osprey Publishing is part of Bloomsbury Publishing Plc.

A CIP catalog record for this book is available from the British Library

Print ISBN: 978 1 4728 0492 1
PDF ebook ISBN: 978 1 4728 0493 8
ePub ebook ISBN: 978 1 4728 0494 5

Index by Fionbar Lyons
Typeset in Sabon
Originated by PDQ Media, Bungay, UK
Printed in China through World Print

15 16 17 18 19   10 9 8 7 6 5 4 3 2 1

Osprey Publishing is supporting the Woodland Trust, the UK's leading
woodland conservation charity, by funding the dedication of trees.

www.ospreypublishing.com

Title page image: SR-71s began operating from RAF Mildenhall, England,
from 1976. Having lined up and completed Exhaust Gas Temperature
(EGT) trim checks, an eerie silence loaded with expectation descended
over the entire airfield while the crew of 61-7964 awaited a green light
from the control tower for a radio silent departure at the beginning of an
operational mission on December 17, 1987. (Paul F. Crickmore)

ACKNOWLEDGMENTS

The material from this book was assembled over 30 years and came
from two basic sources – open literature including books, newspapers,
professional journals, various declassified reports, and first-hand
accounts from pilots, RSOs and other people associated with the Senior
Crown program.

Much of the information contained within these pages was pieced
together during the course of numerous interviews (many of which were
taped, others being conducted over the internet), with those intimately
connected with the Senior Crown program. Several contributed
information with the proviso that their anonymity be respected.

My grateful thanks therefore goes to Col Rich Graham, a good friend
for over 30 years; General Pat Halloran; also Cols Don Walbrecht, Buddy
Brown, Don Emmons, Tom Allison, Ed Payne, Tom Pugh, BC Thomas,
Jerry Glasser, Frank Stampf, Buzz Carpenter, Curt Osterheld, Blair Bozek
and Tom Veltri, also Flt Lt Adam Crickmore, Bob Archer, Tony Landis,
Bob Gilliland, Bob Murphy, Paul Eden, Jay Miller, Jeff Richelson, Mike
Relja, Yefim Gordon and David Allison.

I also wish to thank Cols Tony Bevacqua, Pat Bledsoe, Larry Boggess,
Gary Coleman, Ken Collins, Dave Dempster, Bruce Douglass, Carl Estes,
Tom Estes, Ty Judkin, Joe Kinego, John Kraus, Jay Murphy, Dewain Vick,
Jim Watkins, Rich Young and Jack Maddison; Lt Cols Ben Bowles, Nevin
Cunningham, Bill Flanagan, Jim Greenwood, Dan House, Tom Henichek,
Bruce Leibman, "GT" Morgan, Bob Powell, Maury Rosenberg, Tom
Tilden, Ed Yielding, Reg Blackwell and "Stormy" Boudreaux; Majs Doug
Soifer and Terry Pappas; also Kent Burns, Russ Daniell, Kevin Gothard,
Lindsay Peacock and Chris Pocock.

Thanks too to my editor Tom Milner; and to Neil and Pauline for their
endless support. Last but by no means least my love and thanks go to
Ali, my amazing wife who has been a rock during my recent health scare.

DEDICATION

For my amazing wife Ali

CONTENTS

INTRODUCTION   4

DESIGN AND DEVELOPMENT   5
- A shaky start
- Flight test
- Losses and lessons
- Detachment 6
- NASA

TECHNICAL SPECIFICATIONS   22
- Airframe and layout
- Airframe structure
- Fuel and ignition system
- Engines
- Digital Automatic Flight and Inlet Control System (DAFICS)
- Electrical system
- Hydraulic systems
- Flight controls
- Stability Augmentation System (SAS)
- Astro Inertial Navigation System (ANS)
- Mission Recorder System (MRS)
- V/H, V/R (FMC) system
- Sensors
- Electronic Counter Measures (ECM)
- Crew survival systems

OPERATIONAL HISTORY   38
- Yom Kippur
- Records
- North Korea
- The Iran–Iraq War
- Det 4 operations
- Yemen

THE LONG FAREWELL   55

CONCLUSION   62

BIBLIOGRAPHY   63

INDEX   64

LOCKHEED SR-71 BLACKBIRD

INTRODUCTION

Napoleon Bonaparte once said, "Impossible is a word found only in the dictionary of fools." This ethos could equally have been the mantra of Clarence L. "Kelly" Johnson and his team at Lockheed's so-called Skunk Works, located at Burbank, California, as their aeronautical design and engineering accomplishments pushed at the very boundaries of the barely possible. They were responsible for designing and building the United States' first operational jet fighter, the Lockheed P-80 Shooting Star. This was followed by the legendary F-104 Starfighter – the "missile with a man in it." Next came their ultra-high-flying, reconnaissance-gathering U-2, which 60 years on continues to make immeasurable contributions to the US intelligence community. There then followed the iconic series of Mach 3 plus "Blackbirds" – the Central Intelligence Agency's (CIA's) A-12, the US Air Force's YF-12 interceptor prototype[1] and finally the incredible SR-71.

Designed for sustained triple-sonic flight (2,200mph), at altitudes in excess of 80,000ft (15 miles), the SR-71 – always referred to by the crews that flew it as "Habu," after a poisonous pit-viper found on the island of Okinawa – remains the highest, fastest operational jet ever built, despite having first flown over 50 years ago. The Habu was prematurely retired by the US Air Force and flew its last operational flight on January 18, 1990, during what was at the time an almost obscene rush to slash the defense budget and cash in on the so-called "peace dividend" at the end of the Cold War.

A hint of the high regard in which the Air Force initially held the SR-71 program can perhaps be gleaned from what was its classified codename, Senior Crown. Designed to undertake the role of gathering high-resolution, strategic area reconnaissance of "denied territory," the SR-71's use of extreme speed, altitude and the first application of in-built "stealth" technologies to dramatically reduce its radar cross section (RCS), all combined to vastly increase the platform's survivability in a high-threat environment. Indeed in the early 1960s, when Kelly Johnson allocated the Lockheed internal build numbers, or Article numbers, to the SR-71, he was so confident that the aircraft would remain immune from enemy interception for 40 years, he sequentially began numbering them from 2001.

1   For information on the A-12, the YF-12, and the M-21/D-21 reconnaissance drone platform, see Air Vanguard 12: *Lockheed A-12: the CIA's Blackbird and other variants.*

DESIGN AND DEVELOPMENT

On September 14, 1960, encouraged by the success of his earlier A-12 reconnaissance design for the CIA and the YF-12A interceptor proposal for the Air Force, Kelly Johnson began work on a reconnaissance bomber version of the basic design that he called the RB-12 (RB for Reconnaissance Bomber). In January 1961 he took his unsolicited proposal to Washington and dropped it on the desk of Undersecretary of the Air Force Dr Joseph Charyk. Charyk instructed Col Horace Templeton at the Air Development Center located at Wright Field, Ohio, to conduct an engineering analysis of the proposal. But lacking the required detailed knowledge of integrated bomber systems, Templeton recruited into his team Major Ken Hurley. This proved to be an extremely insightful move, but it placed Hurley in a tricky position as he was instructed to continue with his important "White World" Air Force work on stand-off weapons for the North American RS-70 Reconnaissance Strike bomber (later rechristened the B-70), whilst also working on the "Black World" Lockheed proposal. To further complicate things he was to report in parallel to his boss at the Pentagon, Col David Jones, as well as Col Templeton, whilst under the strictest orders not to inform Jones about his "other job" since Jones wasn't cleared into the program.

Just ten weeks later, Templeton's team took their counter-proposal, which they referred to as the RS-12, back to Charyk, who liked what he saw and instructed them to present it to the Skunk Works boss at Burbank. To his enormous credit, Johnson too was extremely impressed with how the team had enhanced the capability of his original design and, as a result, shelved his RB-12 proposal in favor of the team's RS-12 design.

To provide the Mach 3 bomber with a radar system, the Air Force team had selected two companies to compete for the contract – Westinghouse and Goodyear. It was proposed that each RS-12 would carry a single nuclear weapon internally, which would be based upon the Hughes GAR-9/AIM-47 missile (as carried by the YF-12), and equipped with an adaptation of the Polaris A-3, single megaton warhead. As part of Strategic Air Command's (SAC's), Single Integrated Operational Plan (SIOP), to be implemented in the event of a nuclear war, the RS-12's concept of operations would require the aircraft to penetrate enemy airspace at Mach 3.2 and 80,000ft and use its radar to search designated areas, locate, then identify and strike selected targets. Utilizing its GAM-87 Astro-inertial Navigation System (ANS) that had

The single seat A-12, built for the CIA, was the SR-71's direct predecessor. During the early test phase black paint was applied only to the fuselage chines and wing leading and trailing edges. This reduced thermodynamic heating at cruise speed in addition to hiding the Radar Absorbent Materials (RAM) applied to these areas in order to reduce the aircraft's Radar Cross Section (RCS). This aircraft is pictured outside a hangar at the Area 51 test site. (CIA)

During a meeting held March 16–17, 1960, Kelly Johnson proposed an interceptor version of the A-12 to the Air Force, designated YF-12. Three examples were built and underwent extensive flight-testing. The Air Force was extremely impressed and wanted to order 96 F-12B production aircraft for Aerospace Defense Command, but SecDef Robert McNamara canceled the program on the basis of cost. (Lockheed Martin)

been developed for the subsequently canceled Skybolt ballistic missile, the Air Force and Skunk Works teams confidently predicted that an RS-12, with an all-weather radar-guided missile would be capable of hitting its target within a 50ft circular error of probability (CEP) and just 20ft CEP using an optical system, when launched from an altitude of 80,000ft and a distance of 50 miles.

A Class 1 mock-up of the forward forebody of the RS-12 was built at Burbank and on June 4, 1962, a number of senior Air Force officials travelled to the Skunk Works and reviewed progress to date. However, although this was concluded satisfactorily, a firm commitment to move ahead with hardware wasn't forthcoming. The problem was that the ballistic missile had come of age and considerable doubt was being expressed in some quarters about the long-term viability of bombers as a delivery platform for nuclear weapons. SAC had retired more than 1,500 B-47s from the inventory and President John F. Kennedy had canceled the proposed, high-profile multi-million dollar B-70 Valkyrie bomber on March 28, 1961 (only two prototypes of the large bombers were built for research and development purposes and based at Edwards AFB from 1964 to 1969 – one of the experimental XB-70s was lost following a mid-air collision in 1966). The upshot of all this was that the RS-12 was also never funded and consequently came to nothing. Undaunted, this didn't stop Johnson from submitting yet another unsolicited bomber proposal that he referred to in-house as the B-71, to a small contingent of Air Force generals as late as April 1965, but this too remained a "paper only aircraft."

On December 6, 1962, Kelly Johnson noted in his log, "Working on R-12 *Universal* airplane, using company work order. Can get no decision on any military version of the aircraft, but there does seem to be considerable interest

The mighty (and mightily expensive) North American XB-70 high-altitude Mach 3 bomber ensured that funds were never made available to Lockheed to pursue their RB-12/RS-12 bomber proposal. The XB-70 would also fall victim to budgetary cuts. (General Dynamics via Tony Landis)

in it." Johnson's rationale for this design was based on the premise that if he produced a single platform capable of performing the reconnaissance, recon/strike or intercept role depending on customer needs, it would greatly simplify production, and "It eliminates the necessity of the Air Force deciding which version they want to buy." Seven days later the Skunk Works was visited by several SAC personnel and Johnson logged that "They wanted to see what kind of a reconnaissance version would meet SAC's needs... We prepared our proposal for a 140,000 pound reconnaissance airplane capable of carrying

The SR-71A prototype Air Force serial 61-7950, Article number 2001, was delivered in two sections by truck to Site 2 (Air Force Plant 42, Building 210), at Palmdale, California, on October 29, 1964. (Lockheed Martin)

4,300 pounds of reconnaissance gear and gave it to Col Templeton with a forwarding letter."

One week later, on December 20, Kelly noted that he and several of his engineers flew to Washington to continue their contract pursuit: "Presented our R-12 version, which Templeton and group presented to the Air Force in a closed session the next day. The outcome was that we were proposing too heavy an aircraft, with too much equipment, so we were requested to scale it down to 1,500 pounds of payload."

Further design refinements of the R-12 continued and these were finally rewarded on February 18, 1963, when Lockheed was awarded precontractual authority to build six R-12s, on the understanding that an additional 25 would be ordered by July 1. The first mock-up review of the new reconnaissance aircraft took place on June 13 and 14, 1963, and Johnson noted, "I think the Air Force are well impressed with our operation to this point..." Another mock-up conference took place on December 11, 1963, which was again deemed a success by Johnson. By March 18, 1964, construction was moving ahead rapidly, but contract negotiations with the Air Force had yet to be concluded. Johnson noted in his log, "Spent several days ... on ... the first six R-12s. It is extremely difficult to get a reasonable profit for what we do and no credit is given for the fact we operate more cheaply than the others." Eventually agreement was reached and with an aircraft production rate set at one aircraft per month for 31 months, the entire program was completed under budget at a cost of $146 million (approximately $1.5 billion at today's values); this excluded engines and sensors, but included Categories I, II and III of the flight test program – a remarkable achievement by any standards.

On February 29, 1964, during the run-up to that year's presidential election campaign, and in response to a challenge by Republican candidate Senator Barry Goldwater that the Democrats had neglected the defensive needs of the country, incumbent President Lyndon B. Johnson revealed the existence of the "A-11" (A-12) program. Five months later, on July 25, in yet another piece of electioneering, President Johnson made a second announcement about another hitherto "Black World" aviation program, which in part went:

> I would like to announce the successful development of a major new strategic manned aircraft system, which will be employed by the Strategic Air Command. This system employs the new SR-71 aircraft, and provides a long-range advanced strategic reconnaissance plane for military use, capable of worldwide reconnaissance for military operations.
>
> The Joint Chiefs of Staff (JCS), when reviewing the RS-70, emphasized the importance of the strategic reconnaissance mission. The SR-71 aircraft reconnaissance system is the

most advanced in the world. The aircraft will fly at more than three times the speed of sound. It will operate at altitudes in excess of 80,000ft. It will use the most advanced observation equipment of all kinds in the world. The aircraft will provide the strategic forces of the United States with an outstanding long-range reconnaissance capability. The system will be used during periods of military hostilities and in other situations in which the United States military forces may be confronting foreign military forces.

This is the first known occasion that the R-12 was referred to by its military designation, SR-71. Coming as it did from the President himself, the statement also certainly helped to ensure the aircraft's future survival.

In August 1964, Kelly Johnson phoned Bob Murphy and asked him if he wanted to work on the new reconnaissance aircraft. At the time Murphy was a superintendent in charge of D-21 drone production; he accepted the offer and was immediately briefed by Johnson who said, "I want you to go to Palmdale and get site 2 away from Rockwell [into which North American had merged]. Hire the people you need. The pieces for the aircraft will be up with you on November 1st and I want her flying before Christmas…" At the time, Rockwell controlled all three sites at Palmdale, using Site 1 and Site 3 for XB-70 production. Site 2 housed miscellaneous facilities, including a paint shop and a huge telephone exchange. By bold bluff, Murphy managed to complete the task he was set by Johnson and Lockheed inherited Site 2. On October 29, 1964, two large trailers delivered the prototype SR-71, Lockheed Article number 2001, Air Force serial 61-7950 from Burbank to Site 2, Air Force Plant 42, Building 210 at Palmdale.

In the summer of 1964, Johnson offered Lockheed test pilot Robert J. Gilliland the prestigious post of Chief Project Pilot for the SR-71, a position for which he was eminently qualified, having gained a great deal of experience as a member of the F-104 and A-12 test teams. In December, the two men flew to Palmdale in Lockheed's corporate Jetstar to review progress. Bob Murphy escorted them around building 210 but to Gilliland's great consternation the prototype was still in pieces and spread all over the hangar floor. Gilliland suggested it might be prudent to delay the scheduled first flight until after Christmas, as it was planned that a number of senior Air Force generals were due to witness the event. But Johnson would hear none of it, contending that if he postponed schedules every time he was asked, the aircraft would still be in the jigs!

Through the Herculean efforts of Murphy and his team, the first engine test runs were conducted on December 18, which was followed three days later by a "non-flight." This consisted of full engine checks and culminated in a high-speed run down the main runway at 120kts, before deploying the 40ft brake chute and taxiing back to the hangar. On December 22, 1964, Gilliland got airborne from Palmdale in '950 using his personal call sign, Dutch 51. For safety reasons, the backseat, which would usually carry either a test engineer or an Air Force Reconnaissance Systems Operator (RSO), remained empty. With much of the "pick and shovel work" already

For two months following delivery to Palmdale, '950 was readied for its maiden flight – this is a picture grab from a rare 16mm cine film shot by Lockheed and shows the J58 engines being installed. (Lockheed Martin)

completed by the earlier A-12 and YF-12 test programs, Gilliland was confident enough to take the aircraft up to 50,000ft and Mach 1.5 on this first flight, which was completed as planned and without incident.

A shaky start

In November 1965, the Bureau of Budget (BoB), voiced concern at the costs associated with running both the covert CIA A-12 Oxcart program and the USAF "overt" SR-71 Senior Crown program, and recommended the implementation of a drastic cost-cutting exercise. This entailed closing down the A-12

With Lockheed Test Pilot Jim Eastham flying F-104 chase, Bob Gilliland (using his personal call sign Dutch 51), successfully completed '950's first flight on December 22, 1964. (Lockheed Martin)

program by September 1966. However, Secretary of Defense (SecDef) Robert McNamara rejected the recommendation on the basis of risk, given that the SR-71 wouldn't be mission-ready by that date. However, six months later, a study group was set up specifically to look into reducing expenditure within the two programs. The panel included representatives from the BoB, CIA, and Pentagon, and it identified three possible alternative courses of action, namely: continue running both fleets at current levels; mothballing all A-12s while sharing SR-71s between the CIA and SAC; or – assuming Senior Crown would be ready for operations – ending the Oxcart program in January 1968 and assigning all Oxcart missions to the Air Force. On December 12, 1966, the Director Central Intelligence (DCI) Richard Helms, Deputy Defense Secretary Cyrus Vance, BoB Director Charles Schultze, and presidential scientific advisor Donald Hornig met in Washington and voted three to one that the third option would be recommended to the President – the sole dissenting voice was that of Helms. President Johnson upheld the decision and the CIA began the detailed planning necessary to draw-down Oxcart – even before it had flown a single operational mission. However, as the war in Vietnam escalated, some in the intelligence community claimed that the North were about to deploy surface-to-surface missiles (SSMs). After much prevaricating, the CIA finally managed to persuade the President's special advisory board, known as the 303 Committee, to recommend that Oxcart should be deployed to the SE Asia theater of operations, to verify or dismiss the SSM claims. On May 16, 1967 Helms finally received approval from President Johnson to deploy, whereupon personnel, equipment and three A-12s were flown to Kadena AB, on Okinawa, in support of what was codenamed Operation *Black Shield* – despite the A-12 adhering to a phase-out plan.

Black Shield secured some outstanding reconnaissance imagery during 29 operational missions over North Vietnam, Cambodia/Laos and North Korea. This included enough evidence to conclude that North Vietnam hadn't deployed SSMs. In addition the missions also gained detailed photographic imagery of SAM sites, airfields, naval bases, roads and industrial complexes. This information enabled photo interpreters (PIs), in company with military planners, to develop air defense order of battle estimates, targeting intelligence and bomb damage assessments (BDAs), all of which helped to better develop ingress and egress routes for the vast numbers of US strike aircraft deployed to the conflict. But however vital this role clearly was, it was not what Oxcart had been designed for – namely the penetration of Soviet airspace in order to

Having earlier flown the A-12 on a number of contractor test flights, SR-71 Chief Test Pilot Bob Gilliland was confident enough to take '950 up to 50,000ft and Mach 1.5 on its maiden flight. Gilliland is pictured here in his David Clark S-901 pressure suit. (Lockheed Martin)

collect strategic reconnaissance about their nuclear weapons and industrial capabilities. In effect *Black Shield* was utilizing Oxcart as a tactical collection platform in a conventional military conflict. The policy of limiting A-12 operations in this way was the direct result of the Soviet Union shooting down a CIA-operated U-2 whilst undertaking a clandestine, deep-penetration reconnaissance overflight on May 1, 1960. This action had resulted in successive US presidents publicly committing never again to covertly and willfully violate Soviet airspace with manned reconnaissance aircraft.

By late 1967, and on the back of imagery secured by *Black Shield*, the earlier decommission decision was questioned in some influential circles. The A-12 was lighter and therefore could fly higher than its Air Force stablemate. Additionally, its camera package provided superior ground resolution to those being carried at that time by the SR-71. However, the Air Force countered that its platform carried three different camera packages, and undertook simultaneous synoptic coverage of a target area recording Electronic Intelligence (ELINT) and utilizing its powerful ground mapping radar system to also record Radar Intelligence (RADINT). To try to resolve the dichotomy, a fly-off, codenamed Nice Girl, was staged between the two types and between October 20 and November 3, 1967. An example of each aircraft type flew three identical routes along the Mississippi River. Representatives from a number of interested agencies then evaluated the data collected, but the results were inconclusive. On May 16, 1968, the decision to end the Oxcart program was reaffirmed and the remaining aircraft were flown into storage at Palmdale – the Air Force were now the sole operators of a Mach 3 plus reconnaissance aircraft and the CIA henceforth ceased the direct operation of manned reconnaissance aircraft.

A

SR-71 PROFILES

1: SR-71A prototype 61-7950 first flew on December 22, 1964 from Palmdale, California, with Chief Test Pilot Bob Gilliland at the controls. Unfortunately, the aircraft was written off in an accident during anti-skid brake system trials at Edwards AFB on January 10, 1967.

2: As one of the first six SR-71s to be built, 61-7951 was initially involved in the contractor flight test program. Between July 16, 1971, and September 28, 1978, it was "bailed" to NASA and for political reasons was referred to as a YF-12C. With the serial 06937 on its tail, the aircraft undertook the first of 88 flights with NASA on May 24, 1972. The final flight of '951 was completed on December 22, 1978, having accrued a total of just 796 hours before being placed in storage at Palmdale. When Senior Crown was terminated, it was transported by truck to the Pima Museum, Tucson, Arizona, where it remains on public display.

3: The most striking external modification made to an SR-71 from the operational fleet was that applied to 61-7959. Known, unsurprisingly as "Big Tail" the 8ft 10in. extension was added to house additional sensors and ECM equipment. The aircraft had accrued just 866hrs before Senior Crown was terminated and is now on display at the Air Force Armament Museum, Eglin AFB, Florida.

4: 61-7955 was the backbone of Air Force Logistics Command (AFLC) Det 51/6 at Palmdale, California. Having been placed in storage on January 24, 1985, it reemerged once again in 1991 to be placed on permanent display at the Air Force Flight Test Center Museum, Edwards AFB, California.

Flight test

The first six SR-71s to come off the production line were allocated to the flight test program. Aircraft serials 61-7950, '951 and '952 were Lockheed test vehicles, and '953, '954 and '955 were allocated to the Air Force. In the 1960s Air Force Regulation 80-14 detailed three distinct phases of an Air Force test program. Category I required the contractor, in this case Lockheed, under close observation of the System Program Office (SPO) at Wright-Patterson AFB, to collect and present data to the USAF that proved they were delivering what was ordered; that the aircraft was safe to fly and that its systems functioned in line with the SR-71's mission. Category II testing required Air Force flight test personnel to utilize and apply data provided by Cat I flight testing into a fully integrated, functioning aircraft system that conformed with Air Force operating procedures. Category III flight-testing was conducted at Beale AFB. Here the operational crews and maintenance teams utilized all the data generated in Cat I and II testing, including flight and maintenance manuals and other support equipment, to ensure that it all worked as required in an operational environment and to identify any changes required for further improvements.

Losses and lessons

The first SR-71 to be lost was 61-7952 during a test sortie on January 25, 1966, following an unstart whilst the aircraft was in a 30 degree right bank at Mach 3.1 and 80,000ft. (Lockheed Martin)

Perhaps not surprisingly with such an advanced aircraft, progress to full operational status didn't come easily or without cost. The first SR-71 loss occurred during a test sortie flown out of Edwards AFB by Lockheed test pilot Bill Weaver and his test engineer Jim Zwayer, on January 25, 1966. Aircraft 61-7952 was being flown as per the test card, with its Center of Gravity (CG) positioned further aft than normal to compensate for the rearward shift of the Center of Pressure (CP) encountered at high Mach. This was done in an attempt to reduce trim drag and thereby lower fuel consumption, particularly during the transonic phase of flight. Unfortunately, during a 30-degree banked

turn to the right whilst at 80,000ft and Mach 3.1, the right inlet "unstarted". The cumulative effects of aircraft configuration speed, attitude and altitude resulted in a violent pitch-up and the aircraft disintegrated. Miraculously Weaver survived but Zwayer tragically was killed – his death would prove to be singular amongst all those who flew in the SR-71. The solution to reducing the excessive drag problem was overcome by Kelly Johnson designing and inserting a simple wedge between the aircraft's detachable nose section and its forward fuselage. The external result was a distinctive 2-degree nose-up tilt.

Prototype 61-7950 was written off at Edwards on January 10, 1967, during a maximum gross weight, anti-skid brake evaluation. As the aircraft entered the pre-flooded test section of the runway at over 200kts, Lockheed test pilot Art Peterson shut the throttles and deployed the brake 'chute, which failed to deploy properly. The wheel brakes remained ineffective until the aircraft entered the dry section of the test area, whereupon the brakes locked and all six main tires blew. As momentum carried the aircraft along the runway, the brakes and tires burned out and the wheel hubs disintegrated, causing hot shrapnel to trigger a fire in the fuel tanks. When the aircraft finally came to rest Peterson managed to extract himself. However the aircraft, unlike its pilot, would never fly again.

Lockheed test pilot Bill Weaver (personal call sign Dutch 64) had a miraculous escape following the disintegration of '952. Weaver's back-seater, Lockheed flight test engineer Jim Zwayer, was, however, killed in the crash. (Lockheed Martin)

The first 9th Strategic Reconnaissance Wing (9th SRW) SR-71 loss occurred on the night of April 13, 1967. Shortly after boom disconnect from their KC-135Q tanker, Capt Earle Boone and RSO Capt Richard "Butch" Sheffield began climbing 61-7966 to 30,000ft. The plan was to then execute a standard maneuver for the SR-71, known by the crew force as a "dipsy-doodle." This involved a push-over and a 5,000ft dive before easing back into a supersonic climb – this hastened the aircraft through the highly fuel-inefficient, transonic flight phase. But with the aircraft heavy with fuel, '966's airspeed fell below the required 0.90 Mach. To regain lost momentum, Capt Boone lowered the nose to level flight before again easing back on the stick. This time the aircraft shuddered into an accelerated stall, followed suddenly by a pitch-up rotation from which recovery was impossible. Both crewmen successfully ejected, but for '966, it was the end of the line.

Six months later on October 25, 1967 Beale lost 61-7965. Maj Roy St Martin and his RSO Capt John Carnochan were on a night training flight and on their way back to "home-plate" at Mach 2.8. They'd just eased into the descent profile over central Nevada when, unknown to them both, the gyro-stabilized reference platform for the ANS drifted without a failure warning. Since this system provided attitude reference signals to the primary flight instruments and the autopilot, the crew had no way of knowing on that horizonless night that in fact the aircraft had entered an increasing right bank, while the Flight Director and the Attitude Director Indicator showed no signs of deviating from wings-level flight. The aircraft rolled over and the nose dipped into a steep dive. The first sign the crew had that something was amiss was that the speed greatly increased. A quick look at the poorly located

Two two-seat SR-71B pilot trainers were built; however, the second aircraft, 61-7957 was lost in an accident on January 11, 1968, on approach to Beale AFB. Both crew members ejected safely. (Appeal Democrat via Tony Landis)

standby artificial horizon confirmed to St Martin that they were in a "screaming dive and a roll-over toward inverted flight." Despite his best efforts the pilot was unable to recover the aircraft and they were left with no option but to eject. Luckily both men survived the supersonic ejection as '965 smashed into the ground at high velocity. The subsequent accident board established that pilot error was not a factor in the loss of '965 and recommended a number of design and procedural changes. These included the addition of lights to warn of an ANS failure; that the standby attitude indicator should be both enlarged and placed atop the pilot's instrument panel and that night flying should feature much later in the training syllabus.

Aircraft 61-7957, one of the two SR-71B pilot-trainers, was lost on January 11, 1968. Instructor Pilot (IP) Lt Col Gray Sowers and Capt Dave Fruehauf (on his third SR-71 sortie) suffered a double generator failure near Spokane, Washington. As the weather in the area had closed possible diversion airfields, the crew determined that their best bet was to get to Beale. Their repeated attempts to get the generators restarted all failed so they were forced to shut down all non-essential electrical equipment and rely on the aircraft's batteries. During their long, straight-in approach disaster struck when, at 175kts, the natural 10-degree nose-up angle of attack caused air to be sucked from low-fuel tanks into the fuel-inlet ports. The fuel pumps cavitated, interrupting fuel flow to the engines, and at 3,000ft both engines flamed out. The crew successfully ejected just 7 miles short of home plate. The generators had dropped off-line (as designed) when their power output began to fluctuate slightly, as this situation couldn't be tolerated by the ANS if it was to continue to provide accurate navigational information. As a result of this accident the generator trip parameters were changed, thereby ensuring that they stayed on-line in similar circumstances, as it was rightly felt more important to have an aircraft with an unserviceable ANS rather than no electrical power.

On October 10, 1968, another tire failure on takeoff resulted in the loss of an SR-71, this time 61-7977, crewed by Maj Abe Kardong and his RSO Maj Jim

B **SR-71B**
SR-71B 61-7956 was one of two purpose-built, two-seat pilot trainers. When its sister aircraft, 61-7957, crashed on approach to Beale AFB on January 11, 1968, utilization of this surviving airframe became even more intense – as noted by this paint scheme applied to celebrate the special occasion on January 13, 1982. It is now on public display at the Air Zoo museum in Kalamazoo, Michigan.

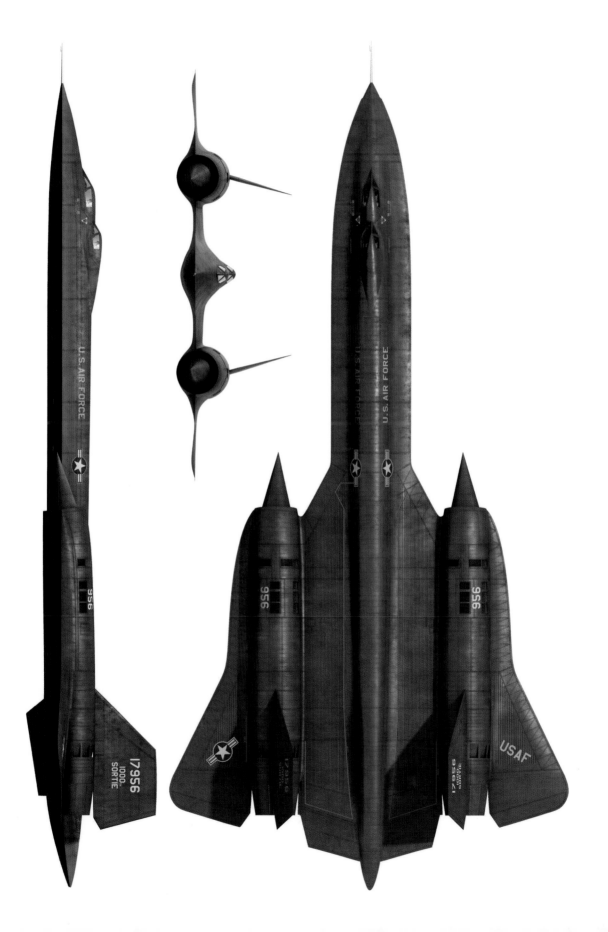

The replacement for '957 was the so-called SR-71C, which utilized the forward fuselage from a static test specimen and the rear section of YF-12A, 60-6934, that had been placed in storage following the cancellation of Project Kedlock. It first flew on March 14, 1969, and was known as "The Bastard" because of its origin and the fact that there was no standard technical data for maintaining the aircraft. (Lockheed Martin)

Kogler. The RSO successfully ejected but Kardong elected to stay with the aircraft and rode '977, minus its undercarriage, some distance into the Beale overrun before the burning aircraft came to a halt. Two crew members rostered for Mobile Control Crew duties that day dashed to the aircraft and helped to safely extract Kardong from the wreckage. Two months after this incident, Category III Operational Testing ended after which the 9th SRW was awarded the Presidential Unit Citation for bringing this highly complex reconnaissance system to operational readiness.

A third tire and wheel incident was responsible for the loss of 61-7954 at Edwards on April 11, 1969, when USAF chief of SR-71 test operations Lt Col Bill Skliar and his RSO Maj Noel Warner suffered left main tire failures at aircraft rotation. With the aircraft at maximum gross weight Lt Col Skliar aborted takeoff, but again the disintegrating wheel hubs punctured the fuel tanks, triggering a huge fuel fire that rapidly engulfed the entire aircraft. Skliar managed to control the aircraft throughout and once the aircraft had stopped both crew members managed to escape. After this incident B. F. Goodrich considerably beefed up the tires, and the issue was resolved.

The fourth and final loss from the original six test aircraft occurred on December 18, 1969, when 61-7953 was on a routine test sortie flown by the Director of the Test Force Lt Col Joe Rogers and his RSO Lt Col Gary Heldelbaugh. This was the aircraft's first flight for many weeks, having undertaken extensive modifications to install a new ECM suite. Having completed air refueling and soon after transitioning to supersonic flight, the aircraft suffered an explosion, loss of power and severe control difficulties which forced both crew members to eject. The crew survived but '953 smashed into the ground in Death Valley – the cause of the in-flight explosion remains a mystery.

On May 10, 1970, over Thailand, having already made one pass over North Vietnam, Maj William Lawson and his RSO, Maj Gil Martinez, began to accelerate and climb 61-7969 away from the KC-135Q tanker from which they'd just completed air refueling (A/R). The weather was particularly bad and they were surrounded by towering cumuli nimbus thunderclouds. Approaching supersonic speed, Lawson eased '969 into a slightly higher climb angle than usual in an attempt to remain clear of cloud and climb over a saddleback at 30,000ft that connected two turrets extending up to 50,000ft. However, heavy with fuel and entering some turbulent cloud, both engines flamed out and the aircraft immediately entered a violent pitch-up maneuver from which there could be no recovery. Both crew members safely ejected and the SR-71 crashed in the vicinity of U-Tapao RTAFB. Heavyweight, accelerated stalls were extremely difficult to recover from and secondary stalls could induce the pitch-up phenomenon, in which the aircraft's angle of attack far exceeded the restorative authority of the flight control surfaces. Not long after this incident an Automatic Pitch Warning (APW) system was added, which proved far superior to the original system, and no further aircraft were lost through stalls.

A freak accident befell 61-7970 and its crew, Lt Cols Buddy Brown and his RSO Mort Jarvis, at 0915hrs on June 17, 1970, when some 20 miles east of El Paso, New Mexico. Brown recalls commenting to Jarvis just how smooth the air was whilst they were on the tanker's boom. Having taken on board 35,000lb of JP-7 fuel, he disconnected and hooked up to a second tanker for more gas. Two or three minutes into the second A/R, the SR-71 crew felt a bump, as if they'd just flown through some turbulent air and both commented on the sensation. Then, following a second small bump, out of nowhere the nose gave a small pitch down before an immediate violent pitch-up that caused the SR-71 to smash into the tail section of the KC-135. The nose of '970 was smashed from the aircraft and Brown's canopy caved in on him. But despite the severe damage, both crew members ejected safely and the '135 managed to limp back to Beale. Brown sustained two broken legs during the ejection but made a full recovery back to flying status.

"The Rapid Rabbit," aircraft 61-7978, was written off at Kadena AB, Okinawa, after an unfortunate landing incident made in high-crosswind conditions just prior to the arrival of a tropical storm on July 20, 1972. The aircraft had its main undercarriage ripped away and broke its back after hitting a low concrete structure adjacent to the runway. Fortunately both crew members, Majors Denny Bush and Jimmy Fagg, escaped unhurt when the aircraft came to a standstill.

The last SR-71 to be written off was aircraft 61-7974, during the course of an operational mission from Kadena on April 21, 1989, when the left engine completely seized whilst at Mach 3 and 75,000ft. It was crewed by Maj Dan House and Maj Blair Bozek. Demonstrating outstanding piloting skill, House retained control of the aircraft, descended and decelerated. However, whilst en route to divert into Clark AFB on the Philippines, he lost all

Lt Col Bill Skliar and his RSO Major Noel Warner had a very close escape when 61-7954 was lost on April 11, 1969, following a burst tire and disintegration of a wheel hub that triggered a massive fuel fire. The problem was solved after B. F. Goodrich beefed up the tires. (Lockheed via Tony Landis)

During the life of the SR-71 program, lessons were invariably learned from accidents and subsequent improvements carried out as a result on the operational fleet. However, the cause of the fire and subsequent loss of 61-7953 on December 18, 1969, remains a mystery to this day. (USAF via Tony Landis)

hydraulic power from the right engine forcing the crew to eject from 15,000ft whilst subsonic, just off the north coast of Luzon. They were initially picked up by some fishermen and then collected from the mainland by a USAF HH-53 Super Jolly Green Giant.

Detachment 6

The SR-71 was in operational service for over 20 years, and during that period many advances were made within the aerospace industry. To provide both logistical support for the SR-71 program and to take advantage of some of these developments, an Advanced Systems Project Office (ASPO) was established at Palmdale. This initially fell under the jurisdiction of Air Force Systems Command (AFSC), but on December 31, 1970, the functions of this unit were transferred to Air Force Logistics Command (AFLC), and Detachment (Det) 51 was created. The unit reported to the Sacramento Air Logistics Center and had sub-division offices at Norton AFB at San Bernardino, California. A further reorganization in September 1977 placed the duties of Detachment 51 (Det 51) at Plant 42 in the hands of Det 6. The unit was manned at any one time by two flight test crews, one drawn from the operational fleet, the other from the USAF Test Pilot School.

Before being incorporated on the operational fleet, any new systems or modifications were first comprehensively tested by Det 51/6. For many years the primary test airframe for such undertakings was 61-7955; however, by 1985, this SR-71 had been so highly modified that it no longer represented the fleet configuration. Therefore, on January 24, 1985, Lt Cols Tom Tilden and Bill Flanagan flew the aircraft on its 722nd and last sortie. It remained in storage until the SR-71 program was terminated and its job at Palmdale was replaced by 61-7972, which was drawn from the operational fleet (this aircraft accumulated 163 test sorties before the SR-71 program was canceled, after which it completed a record-breaking flight by Lt Cols Ed Yeilding and J. T. Vida from Los Angeles to Washington DC in 1 hour 7 minutes 53 seconds on March 6, 1990).

Aircraft 61-7955 was Detachment 6's workhorse. On July 9, 1983, it visited RAF Mildenhall, England, whilst undertaking operational and highly sensitive tests of the new Advanced Synthetic Aperture Radar System II (ASARS II). Well known throughout the military aviation fraternity as "the test bird," '955 had the bogus number 61-7962 applied to its tail to ensure that it didn't attract unusually close (unwanted) attention – the deception worked perfectly. (Lockheed Martin)

Externally, the "Big Tail" conversion carried out on 61-7961 consisted of an 8ft 10in. extension to the tail section. This created 49cu ft of environmentally controlled space into which a 24in. Optical Bar Camera (OBC) and additional, aft-facing Electronic Counter Measures (ECM) could be housed. To facilitate ground clearance during takeoff rotation or flaring for landing, the unit was hinged and moved vertically +/- 8.5 degrees. It was never deployed operationally. (Lockheed Martin)

NASA

On June 5, 1969, a memorandum of understanding was signed between the Air Force and NASA that enabled the latter access to the two remaining YF-12As then in storage. Phase 1 of this program was controlled throughout by the Air Force, and it examined possible bomber penetration tactics that could be adopted against an interceptor touting the capabilities of a YF-12. The program was run from Edwards AFB and terminated on June 24, 1971. Phase 2 consisted of a number of experiments, from testing advanced structures and propulsion studies to correlating wind tunnel data with flight-test data gathered on the aircraft's inlet aerodynamics. Aircraft utilization during this phase of the program proved to be extremely high – especially since the team were down to just one aircraft from June 24, 1971, following the loss of YF-12 60-6936 after an engine fire and subsequent crash whilst on base-leg inbound to Edwards. As a result the Air Force bailed SR-71A 61-17951 to NASA on July 16, 1971, one of the bizarre preconditions being that it was redesignated as a YF-12C. Its serial number was also changed, to 60-6937.

The most ambitious experiment undertaken by NASA whilst operating the SR-71 was the Linear Aerospike SR-71 Experiment (LASRE) project. A total of seven flights took place between October 31, 1997 and November 18, 1998. (Lockheed Martin)

Having completed its 88th test flight with NASA on September 28, 1978, '937 was retired from the program and was followed by '935 on October 31, 1979, after its 145th NASA flight. A week later '935 was ferried to the Air Force Museum at Wright-Patterson AFB, where it was placed on display as the sole surviving example of a YF-12.

In early 1990 NASA once again became involved in operating the SR-71 when it was decided to conduct a number of aeronautical experiments requiring the use of a supersonic test platform. Three SR-71s were placed on loan by the Department of Defense, and in order to comply with Federal Aviation Administration (FAA) regulations, serial numbers were once again changed: SR-71B '956 became NASA 831, and

The final NASA SR-71 test flight team were, top to bottom, Rogers Smith, Ed Schneider, Bob Meyer and Marta Bohn Meyer. (NASA via Mike Relja)

SR-71As '971 and '980 became NASA 832 and 844 respectively. Like the earlier program, this too was conducted from Edwards AFB, and the first of the three aircraft to be readied for flight was NASA 831. The first of three training flights was conducted on July 1, 1991, after which Lt Col Rod Dyckman certified Steve Ishmael as a NASA IP. Thereafter Ishmael checked out a second NASA pilot – Rogers Smith, who in turn flew Marta Meyer and her husband Robert on an orientation flight, as they became the two test engineers on the program.

The most ambitious project to be conducted during this period was the Linear Aerospike SR-71 Experiment (LASRE). Its objective was to provide in-flight data that would enable Lockheed Martin to validate the computational predictive tools it had been using to determine the aerodynamic performance of a future potential reusable launch vehicle. The first of seven flights got underway on October 31, 1997, and during this flight, which lasted 1hr 50mins, aircraft 64-17980 (NASA 844) reached a maximum speed of Mach 1.2 and 33,000ft before recovering back at Edwards AFB. A second flight successfully verified the SR-71/pod configuration, and five further flights were conducted focusing on the experiment. On March 4, 1998, the first of two flights was completed during which time gaseous helium and liquid nitrogen were cycled through the Boeing-Rocketdyne J2-S linear aerospike engine. Three more flights were successfully completed in the spring and summer of 1998, during which liquid oxygen was cycled through the engine. However, numerous cryogenic leaks were discovered, and despite the engine being "hot fired" on the ground on two occasions for a total of three seconds, it was deemed to be too dangerous to fire up the engine with its liquid hydrogen fuel whilst aloft. An investigation into the leaks determined that these would be too difficult and expensive to rectify, and in the event, sufficient information had already been gathered to predict the hot gas effects of an aerospike engine firing during flight; therefore, the program was terminated in November 1998.

The last flight of any SR-71 took place during the Edwards AFB open house weekend of October 9/10, 1999. On the 9th NASA crew Rogers Smith and Robert Meyer flew 61-7980 (NASA 844) up to a speed of Mach 3.21 and an altitude of 80,100ft. Unfortunately it would prove to be its final flight, as the one scheduled for Sunday, October 10, had to be canceled due to a maintenance problem.

 LASRE EXPERIMENT
The LASRE experiment included a 20 percent-scale, half-span model of the X-33 (minus fins) that was rotated through 90 degrees and equipped with eight thrust cells of an aerospike engine. It was mounted on the back of SR-71A, serial 61-7980, NASA 844, via a housing known as the "canoe." The aircraft is now on display at the NASA Dryden Test Center, Edwards AFB, California.

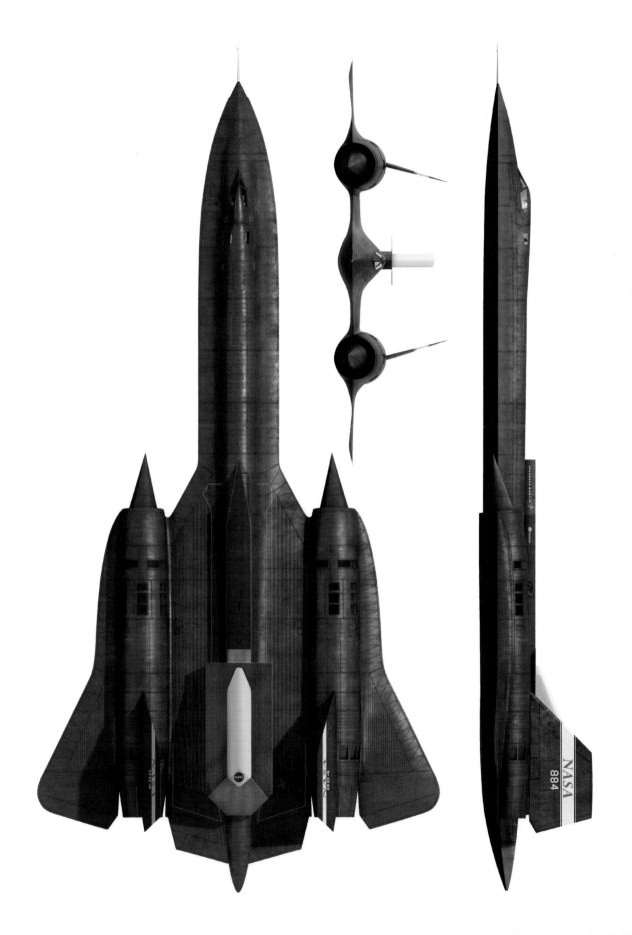

TECHNICAL SPECIFICATIONS

Airframe and layout

The effect of thermodynamic heating brought about by the aircraft's extreme operating envelope was a major factor affecting its construction. Fully 93 percent of the airframe was built from titanium (Beta-120/Ti-13V-11Cr-3A1), while the remaining 7 percent consisted of laminates of phenyl silane, silicone-asbestos and fiberglass to help reduce the aircraft's RCS.

Kirchhoff's law of thermal radiation basically states that a good absorber of heat is also a good emitter, and a good absorber is a black body. By painting the SR-71 black, its surface emissivity value increased from 0.38 for a bare titanium surface, to 0.93, thereby lowering the overall surface temperature by 30 degrees Celsius, a gain thought well worth the 60lb weight penalty.

The SR-71's forward fuselage has a circular cross-section and is of semi-monocoque construction. It housed the pilot and a Reconnaissance Systems Operator (RSO) seated in tandem; the front undercarriage; fuel cells and the air-refueling receptacle. The fuselage sides flare out, creating sharply blended "chines" which produced lift forward of the aircraft's center of gravity (CG), thereby reducing trim drag. Additionally, the chines provided space for equipment bays, and their RAM-covered shape further reduced the aircraft's RCS. The nose section, immediately forward of the cockpit windshield, was structurally independent of the fuselage structure and was interchangeable to enhance mission flexibility. The aft fuselage housed further fuel cells, the brake parachute receptacle and in-flight emergency fuel dump.

The delta wing features two prominent engine nacelles, each mounted at mid-semi-span, and blended into the wing to further reduce RCS. Two rudders mounted on top of each nacelle and canted inboard 15 degrees from the vertical also reduced the aircraft's radar signature. A large, aft-moving spike extends forward from each nacelle, which helped to regulate mass airflow to the two Pratt & Whitney J58 engines. The inlet spikes also helped to shield the engine's compressor face from unwanted radar returns. Additionally, their conical walls were again covered in RAM to reduce RCS.

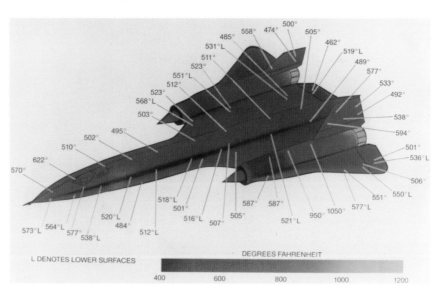

Thermal heating encountered at these values during sustained Mach 3 flight dictated the use of titanium as the primary construction material. (Lockheed Martin)

22

The production facility inside Burbank offers a great opportunity to study the anatomy of the SR-71. In the foreground is aircraft article number 2031, AF serial 61-7980. The forward fuselage forebody is yet to be mated to the aft wing section at joint 715; likewise the outboard wing sections are yet to be positioned. The areas in black are constructed from Radar Absorbent Material (RAM), in order to reduce the aircraft's Radar Cross Section (RCS). Directly behind article 2031 is article 2029, AF serial 61-7978. (Lockheed Martin)

Airframe structure

The wing was arranged into three box sections, one outboard of the engine nacelle and two inboard. The inboard sections were positioned one forward of a 1m-wide compartment housing the main undercarriage bay, the front and rear beams of the inboard box providing support for the main gear. Some 5 degrees of conical camber was applied to the outboard wing leading edge to reduce bending movement, moving most of the aerodynamic load to the rear of the nacelle. The nacelle – an integral part of the wing – acted as a chord-wise beam and torque tube, transmitting and redistributing aerodynamic loads, via the nacelle rings, to the forward and aft inboard wing box sections. The leading and trailing edges of the wings were serrated, the triangular voids being filled with RAM which consisted of a mixture of asbestos and graded dielectric material. This reduced the aircraft's RCS by a method known as "edge softening."

The SR-71 was 107ft 5in. long, had a wingspan of 55ft 7in. and a wing area of 1,605sq.ft. It stood 18ft 6in. high (to the top of the rudders) and its gross weight varied from 135,000lb to over 140,000lb.

Fuel and ignition system

The maximum fuel load weight for the SR-71 was 80,280lb and it was carried in six fuel tanks. Sixteen single-stage centrifugal, AC-powered boost pumps supplied the fuel manifolds. A fuel transfer system controlled the aircraft's CG. A manual forward transfer system together with an automatic and a manual aft transfer system was provided. Built to cruise in after-burner at Mach 3.2 and at altitudes in excess of 80,000ft, the aircraft encountered extremely high airframe temperatures generated by thermodynamic heating. This, coupled with the diverse operating envelope of its Pratt & Whitney J58 engines, required the development of a special fuel which served not only as the source of

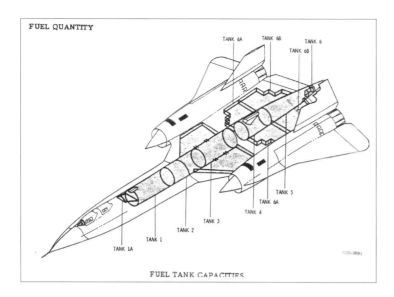

TANK 6A TANK 6B TANK 6
TANK 6B
TANK 5
TANK 6A
TANK 4
TANK 3
TANK 2
TANK 1
TANK 1A

FUEL TANK CAPACITIES

Schematic showing the fuel tank layout. (USAF)

propulsive energy, but also as a hydraulic fluid optimized in the engine hydraulic system to activate the main and afterburner fuel nozzles. In high Mach flight, it was also used as a heat sink to prevent various aircraft and engine accessories from overheating because of the high operating temperatures encountered in this environment. Known as JP-7 (PWA 535), an additive known as PWA 523E was also incorporated into the fuel as a lubricant to aid fuel pump operation. The fuel had high thermal stability so that it wouldn't break down and deposit coke and varnishes in the fuel system passages. High fuel burn temperatures presented the design team with another problem – standard electrical ignition plugs weren't capable of igniting the fuel. To overcome this hurdle, a unique Chemical Ignition System (CIS), using the highly pyrophoric chemical triethyl borane (TEB) was developed. Highly flash sensitive when oxidized, a 600cc tank was carried on each engine and used to start or restart the engines and afterburners on the ground or in the air. At least 16 metered TEB injections could be made from a full tank. To ensure that the system remained inert, gaseous nitrogen was used to pressurize the TEB tank.

To prevent JP-7 fumes in depleted fuel tanks from exploding during high-Mach cruise, because of autogenous ignition from contact with the hot metal skin of the aircraft's "wet-tanks," liquid nitrogen (LN_2) was carried in three Dewar flasks (two containing 106 litres located in the front wheel well and a third containing 50 litres in B bay, in the left forward chine). Nitrogen from the flasks was routed through heat exchangers in tanks 1 and 4 to ensure that it became gaseous and to ensure that the atmosphere in the tanks was 100 percent inert. On the ground, the aircraft was only half filled with fuel and then pressurized using LN_2 to 1.5psi above ambient pressure. Shortly after takeoff the SR-71 would rendezvous with a tanker and get "topped-off." During this process, the LN_2 within the tanks was vented overboard when replaced by fuel, thereby always ensuring that there was a positive head of LN_2 in the tanks. The SR-71's "high-Mach range" was therefore governed by the number of times the aircraft could be refueled before its LN_2 supply was exhausted (the aircraft was limited to a top speed of Mach 2.6 without its tanks being fully inert).

Engines

Power was provided by two Pratt & Whitney JT-11-D20, bleed bypass turbojets (designated J58 by the US military). Designed to operate at Compressor Inlet Temperatures (CITs) in excess of 400 degrees Celsius, each engine developed a maximum uninstalled thrust of 34,000lb in afterburner at sea level. Its single-rotor, nine-stage, 8.8:1 pressure ratio compressor utilized a compressor bleed bypass system at high Mach. When opened, bypass valves bled air from the fourth stage of the nine-stage compressor and routed it through six bypass ducts, around the rear stages of the compressor, combustion section and turbine, before being reintroduced into the turbine exhaust around the front of the afterburner, where it was used to both augment thrust and reduce the Exhaust Gas Temperature (EGT). Transition to bypass operation was scheduled by the main fuel control as a function of CIT and engine speed. This usually occurred within a CIT range of 85–115 degrees Celsius – which corresponded to a Mach range of between Mach 1.8 and 2.0. The bleed bypass process sharply reduced airflow pressures across the rear

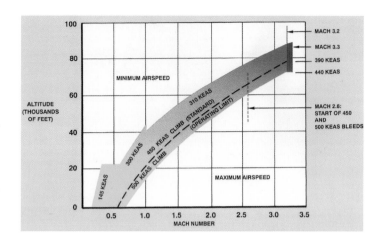

SR-71 performance envelope. (Lockheed Martin)

stages of the compressor assembly and also prevented the front stages from stalling, owing to low mass airflow. The so-called "JY" engines installed on the SR-71 incorporated two-position, movable Inlet Guide Vanes (IGVs), to help guide airflow to the compressor – the A-12s' "JJ" engines had fixed IGVs. These were positioned in either the axial position for takeoff and acceleration to intermediate supersonic speed, or in the cambered position at normal cruise speed. When in the axial position (parallel to the airflow), more thrust was generated. Actuation to the cambered position was controlled by the main engine fuel control and occurred at the same values as those set to activate the bleed bypass process to ensure that the CIT remained within limits (maximum CIT was limited to 427 degrees Celsius). If the IGVs failed to transit to the camber position at Mach 2.0, the checklist called for the mission to be aborted.

The J58 contained a two-stage turbine and its discharge temperatures were monitored by EGT sensors. When at cruise speeds the EGT rose to a staggering 1,100 degrees Celsius. To cope with such extraordinary temperatures, Pratt & Whitney perfected a special high-temperature alloy, known as Astralloy, used in both the first and second stages of the J58's turbine.

Oil supply system

The oil tank was mounted on the lower right side of each engine compressor assembly and contained 6.7 US gallons of oil, designated PWA 524. The engine and speed-reduction gearbox were lubricated by an engine-contained "hot tank" closed system. The oil was cooled by circulation through an engine fuel-oil cooler. The oil was gravity-fed to the main oil pump, which forced oil through a filter and the fuel-oil cooler. The oil was then fed to the engine bearings and gears from the fuel-oil cooler. A pressure-regulating valve kept the flow and pressure relatively constant during all flight conditions. Engine oil temperature was controlled by engine fuel that passed through the main fuel-oil heat exchanger.

Engine fuel hydraulic system

Each engine was provided with a fuel hydraulic system for actuation of the afterburner exhaust nozzle, IGVs, the CIS and the start and bypass bleed valves. An engine-driven pump maintained hydraulic system pressures up to 1,800psi, with a maximum flow of 50gpm for transient requirements. Engine fuel was supplied to the pump from the main fuel pump boost stage.

Access to the J58 engine was via an ingenious hinge arrangement along the top of the engine nacelle. (Paul F. Crickmore)

Accessory Drive System (ADS)

An ADS was mounted forward of the engine in each nacelle. Its three major components included a Constant Speed Drive (CSD), an accessory gearbox and an all-attitude oil reservoir. The ADS received its power from the engine via a reduction gearbox on the engine and a flexible drive shaft. At the ADS, the CSD unit converted the variable speed shaft to a constant rotational speed to power the AC generator. Two hydraulic pumps and a fuel-circulating pump were also mounted on the ADS gearbox. The two hydraulic pumps supplied power for the (A and L) or (B and R) hydraulic systems. The ADS was lubricated by an independent dry sump system with its own pump, drawing oil from the 2-gallon capacity all-attitude oil reservoir. The reservoir was pressurized with nitrogen gas from the aircraft's LN_2 system, and as the term would suggest, it supplied oil to the accessory gearbox, the constant speed drive and the AC generator, regardless of flight attitude.

Air Inlet Control System (AICS)

As explained in detail in Air Vanguard 12, the AICS was a major innovation used to exponentially increase the speed performance of all Kelly Johnson's so-called Blackbirds. Its three elements, the asymmetric mixed-compression, variable geometry inlet; the J58 engine; and the convergent-divergent blow-in-door ejector nozzle, combined to transform the power plant into essentially a "turbo ram-jet" by capturing the supersonic shock wave and using it to create additional thrust.

As the engine was spooled up to 3,200rpm by compressed air, a green flash in the combustion chamber indicated that a shot of Triethylborane (TEB) had done its job and ignited the left J58 engine. (Paul F. Crickmore)

At Mach 1.4, the outlet doors located in the exterior of the engine nacelle began to modulate automatically in order to obtain a prearranged ratio between "dynamic" pressure outside the inlet throat and "static" duct pressure inside the inlet cowl. At 30,000ft, the inlet spikes unlocked and, at Mach 1.6, began moving rearward, achieving their fully aft position at Mach 3.2 – design cruise speed. At this point, despite the throat restriction being 46 percent smaller, the intake's air-capture area had increased by 112 percent (a requirement due to the low ambient air pressure at high altitudes). A peripheral "shock trap" bleed slot stabilized the terminal (normal) shock, and whilst in this configuration the inlet was referred to as being "started." The shock wave was then rammed across the bypass plenum, slowing it to subsonic speed and was forced down a secondary bypass passage, closing exterior nacelle suck-in doors as it went, whilst simultaneously cooling the exterior of the J58 engine, before being exhausted through the ejector nozzles.

With the SR-71 cruising above 75,000ft in ambient air pressures of approximately 0.4lb per square inch and the inlet now generating internal duct pressures of 18lb per square inch, the pressure gradient between the two produced an enormous forward thrust vector which literally pulled the aircraft along. Indeed at Mach 3.2 the inlet generated 54 percent of the total thrust being produced. Bypass air being exhausted through the ejector nozzle produced another 29 percent, leaving the J58 to account for the remaining 17 percent. It's been said that if the pilot were to take the throttles out of the afterburner whilst in this configuration, the engine would actually drag on its mounts!

Impressive as the AICS undoubtedly was, it's not difficult to imagine what happened if this delicate pressure-balancing act was upset, which brings us to another unique Blackbird idiosyncrasy known as the "unstart." With each engine positioned halfway out on each wing, the loss of pressure recovery as the shock wave was "belched" forward from the inlet throat manifested itself in an instant loss of propulsive power and a vicious yaw, in the direction of the "unstarted" engine. When this occurred, the sudden decrease in static pressure was sensed by the AICS and generated an "auto restart" signal. This signal instructed the spike to move forward for 3.75 seconds and the forward bypass doors to open. These actions reduced inlet back-pressure, airflow accelerated and the shock wave was returned to the inlet throat. After the 3.75 seconds had elapsed, the spike and forward bypass doors slowly returned to their scheduled positions – this entire process taking about ten seconds to achieve. To reduce possible catastrophic asymmetric yaw conditions developing at speeds above Mach 2.3, the restart signal was applied to both engines regardless of which inlet had originally "unstarted." In the early days, before the advent of the Digital Automatic Flight and Inlet Control System (DAFICS), these forces were often so strong that crew members had their helmets knocked against the canopy frame – one A-12 pilot had his helmet sun visor smashed.

Digital Automatic Flight and Inlet Control System (DAFICS)

During the mid-1970s mission requirements for the SR-71 increased significantly. Air Force Logistics Command determined that it was both impractical and uneconomical to maintain and repair the aircraft's original analog automatic flight control and engine inlet control systems. To overcome the problem, a three-computer DAFICS was developed to replace the older systems as well as the analog air data computer, the autopilot and the automatic pitch warning system.

TOP The inlet spike regulated the amount of air entering the inlet throughout the SR-71's vast performance envelope by progressively moving rearwards as the aircraft's speed increased. Here the spike is in the fully forward position. (Paul F. Crickmore)

BOTTOM The inlet spike is now at the limit of its 26in. aft translation, showing its configuration at Mach 3 and above. At this point the capture area had increased by 112 percent, while the throat diameter, at the point of minimum cross-section further down the intake, had decreased by 54 percent in order to correctly position the terminal, or normal shock wave. It's interesting to note that at Mach 2.2 the inlet produced just 13 percent of the overall thrust, the engine and ejector accounting for 73 and 14 percent respectively. However, at Mach 3 plus, the inlet generated 54 percent, the ejector 28 percent, and the J58 engine just 18 percent. (Paul F. Crickmore)

Honeywell Corporation was awarded the replacement contract in mid-1978 and aircraft conversion began in August 1980, with the entire fleet having been upgraded by November 1985. At the heart of DAFICS were three Honeywell HDP-5301 digital computers mounted in a single rack. The rack formed a "Faraday Cage" around the computers, protecting them against electromagnetic interference. Each computer had a 16 kilobyte memory (expanded to 32KB in 1987), designated A, B and M. The units designated A and B each had identical software and provided "back up redundancy" for: stability augmentation, autopilot/Mach trim, inlet control, pitch warning, and air data system. The third computer, designated M for monitor, contained built-in test (BIT) software. All three systems had software enabling them to carry out air data computations and stability augmentation in pitch and yaw.

A Pressure Transducer Assembly (PTA) converted pressures from the pitot boom into digital signals, and transmitted this information to the three computers. In the cockpit, a control panel enabled the pilot to make inputs to the stability augmentation and autopilot functions. An onboard analyser interfaced with the M computer to enable maintenance personnel to recall previously stored faults detected by the built-in-tester to carry out checks and adjust inlet schedules.

The SR-71 had a conventional tricycle undercarriage; however, each main gear leg had three tires fitted via a hollow axle. This ingeniously enabled any one wheel to be changed without removing the other two. The tires were made by B. F. Goodrich; the mains were 32ply filled with inert nitrogen gas to a pressure of 415psi, cost about $2,300 each, and were good for 15 full-stop landings. Their walls were impregnated with aluminum powder to reflect heat away from them whilst retracted inside the wheel-well. The front tires didn't require the powder treatment as, once retracted, they were kept cool from air from the Environmental Control System (ECS), being exhausted overboard through the front wheel-well. (Paul F. Crickmore)

Electrical system

Electrical power was normally supplied by two 60kVA AC generators, mechanically driven by their respective engines via the ADS/CSD units and operating in parallel. They provided 115/200 volt, 400-cycle, three-phase power to five AC buses and to two 200-amp transformer-rectifiers – these energized the three 28-volt DC buses. Either generator was capable of supplying the normal AC and DC requirements of the aircraft, thereby providing more than adequate redundancy.

Two 25-amp-hour batteries provided limited emergency power if both generators became inoperative. Maximum duration of the dual-battery power was about 40 minutes, provided that all unnecessary electrical equipment was turned off.

Hydraulic systems

The SR-71 had four separate hydraulic systems, each provided with its own pressurization reservoir and engine-driven pump. Pumps for the A and L system were driven off the left engine ADS. The B and R pumps were powered by the right engine ADS. The A and B hydraulic systems powered the flight controls. The L hydraulic system powered the left engine air inlet system, the landing gear, brakes, air-refueling door and receptacle, in addition to the nose-wheel steering. The R system powered the right engine air inlet system. If pressure in the L system dropped to less than 2,200psi the R system automatically powered the landing gear retraction cycle.

Flight controls

The SR-71 featured elevons mounted along the trailing edge of each wing (these control surfaces acted as both elevators and ailerons to provide control and stability in the pitch and roll axes). Operative power was supplied by the A and B hydraulic systems, and either system was capable of providing sufficient power for control surface operation. Two elevons were located on each wing, one outboard of the engine nacelle and the other inboard. The outboard elevons were slaved to the inboard units. Mechanic stops were incorporated to limit elevon movement for pitch control, thereby ensuring that sufficient differential travel remained for roll control. Total elevon travel was limited to +35 degrees and -20 for the inboard elevons, and -35 degrees for the outboard elevons.

The front cockpit betrays the SR-71's 1960s vintage, with no signs of Color Multifunctional Display Indicators (CMDIs). (Paul F. Crickmore)

The two rudders provided directional control and stability in the yaw axis; their movement occurred by means of a gudgeoned arm positioned by four hydraulic actuators. They were synchronized and moved left or right up to 40 degrees for yaw control.

To avoid excessive aerodynamic loading at speeds above Mach 0.5 that could lead to overstressing the flight control surfaces and the airframe, the outboard elevons and rudders were limited to 20 degrees of movement each side of neutral, and differential elevon travel was limited to 7 degrees. This was achieved by the pilot activating the "Surf Limit" handle, located immediately behind the pilot's control stick. A caution light illuminated if the handle was in the wrong position for the current Mach number.

Stability Augmentation System (SAS)

During normal flight conditions, the SR-71 experienced many changes in attitude due to air loads or control inputs. These attitude changes were sensed by pitch, yaw and roll sensors in each axis (three rate gyros in the pitch axis, three rate gyros plus three lateral accelerometers in the yaw axis, and two rate gyros in the roll axis).

The SAS was a combination of electronic and hydraulic equipment and an integral part of the basic aircraft control system. The SAS was normally engaged in all flight conditions, although it could be disengaged manually. Each axis of SAS (pitch, roll and yaw) was provided with two SAS channels. The SAS detected aircraft attitude changes and initiated control surface deflections to counteract the changes. Normally, the DAFICS A computer ran the A channel in pitch and yaw and the DAFICS B computer ran the B channel in pitch and yaw. The DAFICS M computer would take over the A or B computer, or both, in the pitch and yaw axis should either fail. The M computer drove through servo amplifiers in the A and B computer to provide surface control. The roll SAS was configured so that either A or B computer was

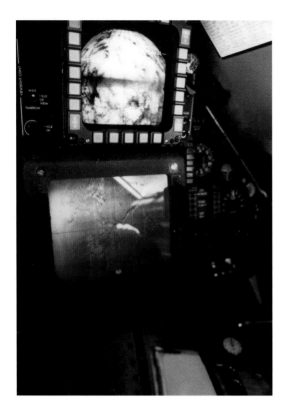

capable of driving both roll servo channels. Sensor and servo monitors provided detection and automatic disengaging capability for faults.

Astro Inertial Navigation System (ANS)

Cruising covertly during operational missions at speeds in excess of a mile every two seconds, it was essential that the SR-71's navigation system was both highly accurate and not reliant upon external navigation aids to ensure the aircraft remained "on the black line." At the heart of successful mission accomplishment therefore was the Nortronics Astro Inertial Navigation System (ANS), designated NAS-142V2. Originally designed for the Douglas Skybolt air-to-surface ballistic missile, which was canceled in 1963, it proved to be a perfect solution for navigating the SR-71 after a few modifications and updates. The system combined data from the inertial navigation platform with a time datum accurate to within five milliseconds. Position updating was achieved automatically by astro-tracking at any one time six of the 52 most prominently visible stars by day or night – in effect using nature as a global positioning system long before GPS was developed. When the autopilot was coupled to the ANS via the AutoNav function, the SR-71 could be flown automatically, adhering precisely to a predetermined flight path that was loaded pre-flight into the ANS's computer memory. The ANS was backed up by a Singer-Kearfott (SKN-2417) Inertial Navigation System (INS) that had a circular error of probability (CEP) of just one nautical mile for every flight hour.

The RSO's view-sight display can be seen at the top of this photograph, with the Synthetic Aperture Radar (SAR) display screen positioned immediately below it. When reequipped with the Advanced Synthetic Aperture Radar System II (ASARS II), the SR-71 was used extensively to reimage target areas with the high-resolution system, which of course worked effectively through cloud cover. (Lt Col Curt Osterheld)

Mission Recorder System (MRS)

The MRS recorded and stored up to 12 hours of system performance data, which included maintenance information and actions of the sensors and navigation systems, in addition to all inter-cockpit and radio voice transmissions.

 SR-71 PROFILES

1: The significance of this particular piece of tail-art is unfortunately unknown; therefore one can only speculate that maybe the baby of one of the maintenance technicians or crewmembers was not the easiest child to raise! It was seen whilst 61-7980 was deployed to Det 1, at Kadena on September 18, 1969.

2: SR-71B 61-7956 whilst serving with NASA as serial 831 between July 1991 and October 1999.

3: SR-71A 61-7962 completed the final flight of its full and active career on February 14, 1990, having accrued a total of 2,836 flight hours. It is the only SR-71 to be found in a museum outside the United States, and it is appropriate that it is at the Imperial War Museum, Duxford, England, just a one-hour drive from the ex-home of Det 4, RAF Mildenhall.

4: SR-71A 61-7972 on March 6, 1990, after its retirement and record-breaking flight from the west to east coast of the United States. Flown by Lt Col Ed Yeilding and his RSO Lt Col J. T. Vida, this historic aircraft also holds the current world speed record from New York to London and from London to Los Angeles. It is on permanent display at the Smithsonian Air and Space Museum.

1

2

3

4

V/H, V/R (FMC) system

The V/H (Velocity/Height ratio) or FMC (Forward Motion Compensation) system provided signals through the V/H bus system to the cameras to improve their photographic resolution. The signals caused the camera mirror or film platen to move in such a way that the terrain imaged below remained stationary on the film during exposure while the aircraft moved forward. The voltages, scaled at 0.2 volts (DC), represent the angular rate of aircraft forward motion relative to the terrain directly below.

The V/R (Velocity/Radial) distance was another value used to drive the camera's motion compensation mechanism, based upon the actual distance to the target to be photographed. For example, when the SR-71's TEOCs were looking out at an angle of 45 degrees, the distance to the target was significantly greater than its altitude above the ground and therefore required an element of FMC. V/R was also used when the aircraft was in a turn and was particularly useful during the Vietnam War to peer into caves. The V/H or V/R signal could be set manually by the RSO but in practice this was usually done by the ANS. The units of motion used were milliradians per second (mr/sec). This was calculated by dividing the aircraft's true airspeed by its altitude; as an example, at 1,850 Knots True Airspeed (KTAS), and 77,500ft elevation, V/H = 42 mr/sec.

Sensors

The essence of the SR-71 was to provide a survivable platform from which its sensors could be utilized to monitor (sometimes from within "denied territory"), the military activities of a foreign power(s). Therefore, at the very heart of the Senior Crown mission was its sensor package, which was required to operate effectively and reliably throughout the aircraft's extreme performance envelope: otherwise, in the words of Col Roy Stanley III, commander of the 67th Reconnaissance Technical Squadron, "the aircraft would just be burning expensive holes in the sky." The sensors developed for the SR-71 were continually improved during the aircraft's lifetime and are detailed here as those equipping the SR-71 at the end of her career – they were all nothing short of awesome.

Nose sensors

To facilitate maximum mission flexibility, the SR-71 featured three interchangeable nose sections housing either a high-resolution, side-looking radar (SLR), used for ground mapping and referred to as CAPRE – standing for Capability Reconnaissance Radar; an Advanced Synthetic Aperture Radar System (ASARS) – or a so-called "glass-nose" housing a palletized Optical Bar Camera (OBC).

Both the CAPRE and OBC units were mounted within nose sections featuring silicone-asbestos chine panels. Manufactured by Loral, from mid-1972 these units began replacing an earlier, less capable system known as PIP. This synthetic SLR could be used in conjunction with the Radar Correlated Display (RCD), located in the center of the RSO's front console, to produce an in-flight display for navigation purposes. However, its main function was to illuminate ground targets that were then recorded onto a filmstrip 1,300ft in length by two recorders housed in the aft portion of the right forward mission bay. The unit could be programmed to cover a strip either 10 or 20nm wide either side of the aircraft's track.

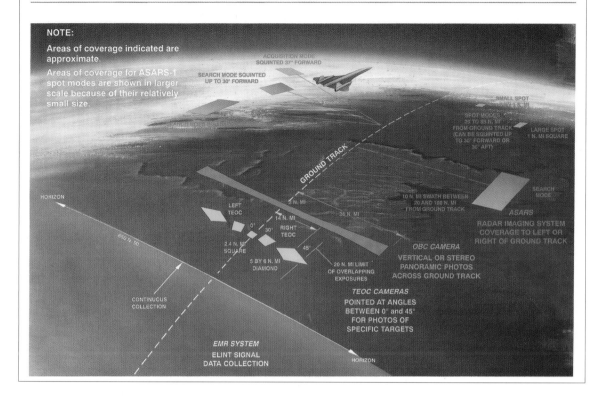

NOTE:

Areas of coverage indicated are approximate.

Areas of coverage for ASARS-1 spot modes are shown in larger scale because of their relatively small size.

ACQUISITION MODE
SQUINTED 37° FORWARD

SEARCH MODE SQUINTED
UP TO 30° FORWARD

SMALL SPOT

SPOT MODES
20 TO 85 N. MI
FROM GROUND TRACK
(CAN BE SQUINTED UP
TO 30° FORWARD OR
30° AFT)

LARGE SPOT
1 N. MI SQUARE

GROUND TRACK

HORIZON

650 N. MI

LEFT
TEOC

14 N. MI

0° 30° RIGHT
TEOC

2.4 N. MI
SQUARE

45°

5 BY 6 N. MI
DIAMOND

5 N. MI

36 N. MI

20 N. MI LIMIT
OF OVERLAPPING
EXPOSURES

10 N. MI SWATH BETWEEN
20 AND 100 N. MI
FROM GROUND TRACK

SEARCH
MODE

ASARS
RADAR IMAGING SYSTEM
COVERAGE TO LEFT OR
RIGHT OF GROUND TRACK

OBC CAMERA
VERTICAL OR STEREO
PANORAMIC PHOTOS
ACROSS GROUND TRACK

TEOC CAMERAS
POINTED AT ANGLES
BETWEEN 0° and 45°
FOR PHOTOS OF
SPECIFIC TARGETS

CONTINUOUS
COLLECTION

EMR SYSTEM
ELINT SIGNAL
DATA COLLECTION

HORIZON

Loral's ASARS was mounted in a nose section of full monocoque construction that consisted of astroquartz and polymide to optimize X-band transmissivity. It was first deployed operationally to Det 4, located at RAF Mildenhall, on July 9, 1983. The technology catapulted radar-generated ground-mapping into a new dimension, providing a resolution at nadir (a point on the ground directly below the aircraft) of less than 1ft from 80,000ft. The radar imagery was recorded onto a tape 9,220ft in length: furthermore this digitized information could be transmitted from the aircraft during the mission to a ground receiving station in near-real time (unfortunately, as will be seen later, the Air Force failed to capitalize on this capability leap).

The other nose-mounted sensor was the OBC; an earlier version equipped with a 24in. focal length lens was replaced from November 1973, by units toting a 30in. lens. Built by the Itek Corporation, the lens system featured a fixed aperture mounted on an "optical bar" that accommodated the lens and two mirror assemblies used to create a folded optical path, which reduced the physical size of the package. The camera was not stabilized, but had vibration isolation and damping. The optical bar revolved continuously around its longitudinal axis whenever power was applied. Film exposure was accomplished through a scanning slit shutter while the bar and film were in motion. Aircraft FMC was achieved using a "nodding" mirror, and was automatically provided during frame exposure when the V/H ratio was between 35 and 45mr per second; otherwise, the FMC was set automatically at 40mr per second if the applied signal fell outside that range. The exposed scan angle was 140 degrees, i.e. 70 degrees either side of the SR-71's track, with a field angle along the flight path of approximately 8 degrees. A data

This schematic shows the "ground print" of the various sensor systems with which the SR-71 could be equipped. (Lockheed Martin)

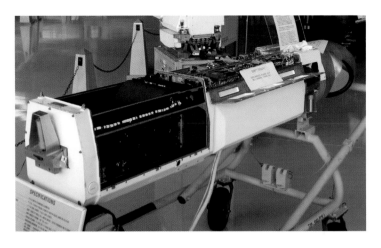

The beryllium mirror located in the scan-head (furthest from camera), provided both forward motion compensation and could tilt to angles of up to 45 degrees from the SR-71's track to search-out pre-programmed targets, enabling the Hycon HR-308's 48in. focal length lens to obtain outstanding "close-look" photography. (Greg Goebel)

block was applied to each frame recording mission information, frame number and camera fore/aft or vertical orientation. Two types of black and white film were used, designated 3414 or 1414. It was extremely slow, with an ISO rating of just 8, providing the photographic interpreters with image resolution at nadir of less than 1ft.

The SR-71 could also be configured to carry two "close-look" Hycon Technical (TECH) or Technical Objective Cameras (TEOCs). There were two models available: the HR-308B and the HR-308C. The HR-308B came in two versions, the -11 and the -21. Except for passive vibration isolation, the HR-308B was unstabilized, while the HR-308C was actively stabilized in pitch, roll and, at higher look angles, in yaw. Each camera was mounted horizontally and viewed targets below and out to about 45 degrees by tilting a beryllium mirror located in the camera's scan-head. It was the only camera carried by the SR-71 that was capable of being pointed at different angles. The camera's 48in. focal length lens imaged onto fine-grain film, producing a 9½sq in. frame. Maximum film capacity was 1,500ft, producing 1,800 usable frames per camera. The normal ground area being photographed was about 2½ square miles per frame. FMC is obtained by rocking the camera's head at a variable rate determined by V/R (velocity divided by slant range). These narrow-field framing cameras had four modes of operation: "Burst Mode" took a burst of ten photos at a rate of about one per second, while "Stepping Mode" slewed the camera head back and forth, four digits either side of a command look angle. This provided wider coverage of a given area when the target's precise location was unclear or covered a larger area on the ground than the normal frame width. Finally, two overlap modes were available. One was timed to provide a 55 percent overlap of each consecutive frame; the other produced a 10 percent overlap between frames. The package was activated either automatically by the ANS or manually by the RSO. It's disappointing to note that despite the considerable passage of time, to date no operational imagery (other than a couple of frames released to the press following the raid against Libya in April 1986) has been declassified by the Air Force (unlike imagery declassified by the CIA's A-12 Oxcart program).

SIGINT Receivers

Once activated by the RSO, the Electromagnetic Reconnaissance System (EMR) was an entirely automatic, passive collection system and performed two search functions simultaneously: special search and general search. Special search was based upon preflight instructions in the ELINT Improvement Program (EIP) system computer that designated emitters of special interest. When a received signal matched the designated emitter, a monitor receiver was automatically tuned to that signal for a pre-programmed period, and the signal pulses were passed to special detectors and recorded on tracks of the continuous analog recorder as video signals to be evaluated utilizing specialist equipment after landing.

The general search function searched the frequency spectrum from 30MHz to 40GHz. This spectrum was divided into six bands, all of which were searched simultaneously. Every emitter signal received in the bands was recorded on the digital recorder by way of time, frequency, direction, pulse width and amplitude.

The continuous analog recorder was a 14-channel Ampex Model AR-1700 wide-band magnetic tape recorder that recorded special search signals, ELINT data from the on-board DEF systems, and maintenance data. The recorder could be operated automatically by the EIP system and/or manually by the RSO.

The tape transport operated at 5 or 10ft (1.5 or 3m) per second. A 14in. (35.6cm) reel supplied 9,200ft (2,804m) of 1in. (2.5cm) magnetic tape that provided 30 or 15 minutes of recording time per flight, depending on the recording speed selected.

Electronic Counter Measures (ECM)

The SR-71 did not carry any form of defensive weaponry save that which was generated electronically. ECM was and remains a highly sensitive area, where fast-moving technological advances meant that the SR-71's Defensive Electronic systems (DEF) required continual updating throughout its operational life. The controls required to operate all the DEF systems were located on a single panel on the RSO's left console, an arbitrary alpha-numeric system was used to identify equipment fit, and at the time of its retirement, the aircraft was equipped with systems A2, C2, H and M.

A2 was an ECM jammer system designed to protect the aircraft from airborne threats operating in the X-band frequency band. It consisted of two sets of receive and transmit antennas, and a gaseous nitrogen system to pressurize the transmit waveguides. The receive antennas were located in "blisters" on the left and right sides of the nose chine and identified the threat as coming from below the aircraft in either the left or right forward quadrants. A2's transmit antennas protruded slightly from the lower surfaces of the chines, opposite the pilot's cockpit. The DEF A2 system was interfaced with the MRS, radar and EMR system and when mission requirements dictated, the received signals could be recorded for later analysis on the AR1700 recorder.

C2 worked in conjunction with DEF H to protect the SR-71 from the SAM threat. It consisted of a receiver, band antenna, band-pass filter, power relay, and electrical and coaxial cables. On receipt of a signal received from DEF C2 the DEF H system was triggered into operation.

Carried in compartment bay K and weighing in at 900lb, DEF H was an extremely powerful piece of kit that provided threat warning and, when required, barrage noise jamming for protection against the SAM threat. It included a transceiver, two transmitting systems, an interface unit (IU), a data processor and an evaporative cooler. Radar signals associated with the various SAM threats (essentially the SA-2 or

The Electronic Counter Measure (ECM) system named DEF H was an extremely effective and powerful noise jammer. (Mike Hull)

Had the powers that be continued to fund the SR-71 program with its updated sensor system, the data link antenna housed in this dome would have enabled its digitized reconnaissance data to be downloaded, processed and in the hands of military and political leaders in near-real time. (USAF)

SA-5) were captured by two sets of receivers. Those signals, received by a forward centerline antenna, were sent to the transceiver. Signals received by an aft centerline antenna were routed to the DEF H system through a band pass filter and preamplifier. The IU controlled the jamming pulses generated by the transmitting systems. The transmitting systems were designated as low band or high band and each band could be driven by commands from the DEF control panel. Upon receipt of signals from DEF C2, DEF H transmitted on frequencies predetermined by the LO and/or HI band selections on the RSO's DEF console. Signals received by DEF H could if required be recorded on the AR1700 recorder for later analysis.

DEF M is a deceptive repeater jammer ECM system utilizing two techniques known as Velocity Gate Pull-Off (VGPO) and Range Gate Pull-Off (RGPO). The specific threat that DEF M operated against (SA-2 or SA-5) remains classified. What we do know is that DEF M utilized a single antenna located on the aircraft's underside centerline forward of the RSO's view sight where it was protected by a slightly protruding fiberglass radome and was time-shared between its receive and transmit functions. Jamming continued for five seconds after the threat was no longer present.

Range Gate Pull-Off (RGPO)

If barrage noise jamming is the ECM equivalent of taking a sledgehammer to crack a walnut, then RGPO is the essence of surgical finesse. Basically, when a tracking radar has detected its target, it brackets it with range gates. These essentially blank out all other signals that originate from outside the narrow "window" the gates have created, thus increasing the signal-to-noise level ratio. The radar then "focuses" on a range interval of just a few hundred meters that frames the target's location, and no longer attempts to detect other targets. This state of affairs is known as radar "lock-on." But range gates can be hijacked, causing the radar to break lock, and this is precisely what RGPO does.

Firstly the RGPO jammer determines the incoming radar's pulse repetition frequency (PRF). It then amplifies and retransmits it back when further pulses are received. Highlighting itself on an enemy's radar screen in this way hardly seems like a good idea; however, the jammer progressively increases its power, creating in the process a much stronger return than that generated from the aircraft itself. The sensitivity of the tracking radar's receiver has to then be reduced to avoid overload. As a consequence, the aircraft's actual return echo is immersed and vanishes below the "noise floor." The RGPO jammer now transmits a second replica "return" after each of the "dummy" echoes. The power of this second replica return is again increased while the dummy is made weaker. At this point, the tracking radar locks on to the now stronger second replica return, which the RGPO jammer begins to delay by small, but ever increasing, amounts of time. The radar's range gates follow the dummy target, which appears to be receding. This continues until the radar's range gates have moved away from the target's true position, thereby causing the radar to track a "phantom target." Now the aircraft's actual return is blanked out entirely by the range gates. The RGPO jammer then switches off, leaving the radar with nothing but noise between its range gates. The deception has worked and the radar lock has been successfully broken. This now requires the radar to revert back to search or acquisition mode, whilst all this time the SR-71 has been speeding away from the radar head at a rate of one mile every two seconds. Countermeasures to RGPO are available – switching to another PRF, for example, renders the jammer incapable of anticipating the timing of the next illuminating pulse. There are also other methods too, as well as counter-countermeasures to these, but they fall outside the scope of this book.

Crew survival systems

Within the SR-71's cockpit, pressurization was allowed to fall steadily as the aircraft climbed from sea level to 8,000ft, whereupon it remained constant to 25,000ft. Between these altitudes the ambient air pressure fell from 10.9psi to 5.9psi respectively, producing a pressure differential of 5psi. This maximum figure was maintained by the aircraft's pressurization system throughout the aircraft's entire flight profile. This ensured that the fuselage wasn't subjected to unduly high pressure gradients, which in turn meant that the aircraft's structural weight could be reduced. However, if pressurization was lost or the crew needed to eject, survival was dependent upon each of them wearing a full pressure suit. This requirement was reinforced by Air Force regulation 60-16 which stipulated that full pressure suits must be worn when flying above 50,000ft.

Like most other systems associated with the SR-71, the pressure suit evolved throughout the life of the program. The first suits designed for the SR-71 program were designated S-901J. These varied from those designed for the A-12 and YF-12 crew members, since they were non-custom-built and instead were available in 12 standard sizes, the first being produced in 1965. Initially the outer coveralls of these early suits had a layer of aluminum vacuum-deposited on HT-1 material, to provide a level of fire-resistant protection during high-Mach ejection and to help reflect heat away from the crew member when in the cockpit – the inner surfaces of the windows routinely reached temperatures of 120 degrees Celsius. The problem with this was that the suit generated unwanted reflections, making it difficult for the crew to monitor instruments. A white coverall was developed that reduced, but did not eliminate, the problem. The drawback here was that the white Dacron material from which the coveralls were made was not fireproof. David Clark therefore developed a material called Fypro. Its dark chocolate-brown color killed unwanted cockpit

SR-71 pilot Major Tom Danielson makes his way to the recliner within the Physiological Support Division (PSD) "bread-van" that transported crew members from the suit-up facility to their waiting jet. He's wearing the S1030 pressure suit. (Paul F. Crickmore)

KALMBACH PUBLISHING CO.
DAVID P. MORGAN MEMORIAL LIBRARY
P.O. BOX 1612
WAUKESHA, WI 53187-1612

reflections, but did nothing to reflect internal cockpit heat away from the crew. In 1977 the company developed the next generation of pressure suits, designated the S-1030 series and featured a high level of commonality between the U-2 and SR-71 programs. Colored "Old Gold" the suit incorporated state-of-the-art textiles and was more durable and comfortable. Its four principal layers consisted of an outer coverall of Nomex that was durable, tear and fire resistant. It contained zippered pockets on the upper and lower legs, Velcro patches on the upper legs to secure checklists, and the parachute harness connections. The next layer acted as a restraint/pressure boundary layer and consisted of tightly woven mesh netting that became more rigid and contained the expansion of the third layer if it inflated and pressure increased. A third layer, called the bladder, performed rather like a tire inner tube and was made of a rubber compound which would inflate with loss of pressurization or upon ejection, thereby protecting the crew member. Finally, an inner scuff layer made from lightweight Dacron material (a form of Terylene) protected the all-important bladder layer from scuffing against the skin or other clothing. A urine collection device (the UCD) enabled crew members to urinate and remain dry, whilst maintaining suit pressurization. An optional thermal layer could be worn inside the suit, but this was usually discarded in favor of more comfortable long john cotton underwear, which was worn inside out, to prevent the seams from pressing into the skin.

The S-1030 suit was also manufactured in 12 different sizes and it assumed the seated position when pressurized, to aid cockpit mobility. The helmet, designated GN-121394, was attached to the suit via a roller-ball ring to enable the head to be turned. Oxygen was supplied to the crew members through holes situated around the helmet face-seal. A bailer-arm locked the clear face visor in place to ensure that an airtight seal was maintained at all times, and an outer tinted visor was also incorporated as a sunshield. An airtight port located on the lower right side of the helmet enabled crew members to drink water via a straw to ensure they remained hydrated, and a level of sustenance was also available in the form of liquidized food dispensed from a tube. This was made by Gerber, the baby food manufacturer! Gloves completed the pressure seal and were attached via wrist hinges. Boots featured heel retraction strips that were connected by cable to the ejection seat on entry to the cockpit. The complete pressure suit system cost about $130,000 a copy. Crews were issued with two and they lasted 10–12 years, undergoing a complete strip-down overhaul every five years and a thorough inspection every 90 days, or 150 hours.

OPERATIONAL HISTORY

On December 14, 1964, five months after President Johnson announced the existence of the SR-71, eight days before the jet's first flight, and whilst all the in-fighting still raged between the BoB, CIA and SecDef over which aircraft program should be axed (the A-12 or the SR-71), General John Ryan, Commander-in-Chief of Strategic Air Command (CINCSAC – pronounced SINK-SAC), announced that the SR-71 would be operated by the 4200th Strategic Reconnaissance Wing and activated at Beale AFB, California, on January 1, 1965. (Beale AFB remained the home of the SR-71 throughout its operational life and was where all crew training was conducted; however, only a relatively few operational missions were flown from the base.)

Following an $8.4 million military construction program to bring the base up to scratch, the first of eight Northrop T-38 Talons arrived for crew proficiency training on July 7, 1965. Col Doug Nelson, the 4200th Wing Commander, together with Instructor Pilot Lt Col Ray Haupt, delivered Beale's first SR-71 – a B model, on January 7, 1966. This was followed shortly thereafter by the second B model; however, it wasn't until May 10, 1966 that the wing's first A model arrived and the steady build-up of operational aircraft got underway.

Col Doug Nelson, commander of the 9th SRW (second from right) takes delivery of the first SR-71B from Bob Murphy, Plant Manager at Site 2, Palmdale, on January 6, 1966. (Bob Murphy)

The classified and sensitive nature of gathering global strategic reconnaissance, sometimes from "denied" areas, meant that such activities had to be highly regulated. It was therefore logical that SAC was the program's command authority, as it was both a major command of the USAF and a Joint Chiefs of Staff (JCS) specified organization. Headquarters USAF assigned to SAC the responsibility of conducting all strategic reconnaissance operations, and the command executed this mission under the supervision and guidance of the Chief of Staff, USAF. The CINCSAC was tasked to direct and prepare plans for strategic aerospace reconnaissance for which the Air Force is responsible in order that global requirements of the Department of Defense (DOD) can be met.

Requirements for individual reconnaissance programs were specified and outlined in operations and fragmentary (frag) orders, and fielded through the Strategic Reconnaissance Center (SRC), at Offutt AFB, Nebraska. Headquarters SAC exercised operational control over all such missions, supervising their planning, scheduling and execution, unless such functions had been specially delegated in a SAC operational order.

Specific SR-71 operations were planned by specialists within the SR-71 branch of the SRC in response to tasking by the JCS, initially in support of SAC's SIOP (the nuclear deterrent), the Defense Intelligence Agency (DIA), the Commander in Chief Pacific (CICPAC), Seventh Air Force, Military Assistance Command Vietnam and US Air Forces in Korea (COMUSKOREA). Senior Officers at the SRC participated in twice-daily meetings at 0730hrs and 1530hrs to review the current mission tasking, planning and weather situation. Once the SRC had completed the mission planning process, details were forwarded to the JCS for final sign-off.

On June 25, 1966, the 4200th SRW was redesignated the 9th Strategic Reconnaissance Wing, and its subordinate squadrons became the 1st and 99th Strategic Reconnaissance Squadrons (SRS) – the 99th SRS was deactivated as an SR-71 unit in March 1971, after which its assets were transferred over to the 1st SRS.

When the decision was finally reached to terminate Oxcart and replace it with the Senior Crown program, 9th SRW crews began preparing for the

ASPEN was the radio callsign used for all stateside SR-71 training sorties; the two-seat SR-71B always used ASPEN 39, while "A" model flights started with the number 30 and ran consecutively throughout the day. Here ASPEN 31 draws back from the tanker, having completed a full fuel off-load over the Rockies. (Paul F. Crickmore)

trans-Pacific deployment to Kadena AB by flying long-haul stateside training sorties. The three-ship, A-12 reconnaissance mission of North Vietnam, codenamed *Black Shield*, would be replaced initially by three SR-71s operating under a 9th SRW detachment, initially designated Operating Location 8, or OL-8. During 20 years of SR-71 operations from Okinawa, the detachment was redesignated OLRK on October 30, 1970, and then OLKA on October 26, 1971. It finally became Detachment 1, or Det 1, of the 9th SRW in August 1974, a title it then retained until 1990 when the SR-71 fleet was retired.

Two days before the deployment to Kadena AB, six KC-135Q tankers were positioned at Hickham AFB, Hawaii, to provide air refueling support during the trans-Pacific flight. Deployment to OL-8 began on March 8, 1968, under the codename Glowing Heat (the codename used whenever SR-71s were deployed from Beale) with aircraft '978. This was followed two days later by '976, and finally by '974 on March 13. A fourth crew arrived three days later, having been deployed in theater by KC-135Q tanker. It was whilst at Okinawa that the SR-71 received its nickname, Habu, after a dark, poisonous pit viper, indigenous to the Ryukyu island chain. Although "Blackbird" has long been the name publicly associated with the SR-71, it's a title shunned by crew members.

Prior to departure from Beale, it had been agreed that the first crew to arrive on Okinawa would also be the crew that flew the first SR-71 operational sortie. However, because of maintenance problems, that accolade slipped to Majors Jerry O'Malley and Ed Payne in aircraft '976. The mission was flown on March 21, 1968, and the route followed that of the first *Black Shield* A-12 sortie, ten months earlier. For this historical first operational mission, '976 was configured with a Goodyear Aerospace GA-531 high-resolution radar (HRR) in the nose section. A Fairchild Camera Company F489 Terrain Objective Camera (TROC) was mounted in equipment bay C. Next came two close-look HR-308B TEOCs and finally two Iteck Corporation HR-9085 Operational Objective Cameras (OOCs), mounted in bays S and T.

The post-mission reconnaissance "take" was stunning. The HRR results revealed the location of heavy artillery emplacements around the besieged outpost of Khe Sanh, and a huge truck park used in support of the guns; both sites had managed to elude previous US recce sorties up to that time. Within the next few days, air strikes were mounted against both targets, reducing their effectiveness dramatically. After a 77-day siege, Khe Sanh was at last relieved on April 7, 1968 (two weeks after '976's "discovery" sortie). As a result of their significant contribution to this highly successful mission, O'Malley and Payne were each awarded the Distinguished Flying Cross (DFC). On its very first operational sortie, the aircraft had proven its value and it would continue to do so on many hundreds of other occasions over the coming years.

Several early OL-8 operational missions over North Vietnam were aborted in flight owing to problems involving the SR-71's generators dropping off-line. This often led to aircraft having to divert into one of the USAF bases in Thailand. Once on the ground, the generators mysteriously worked perfectly. Some diligent detective work by the aircraft's outstanding maintenance technicians eventually identified the problem, which was caused by thermal heating. Immersed in a "thermal thicket" at high cruise speed, solder that secured wires to the generators melted. When back on the ground the aircraft cooled, the solder solidified and the generators worked. Once identified the fix was simple: the wires were reconnected using solder with a much higher melting point. Of the 168 SR-71 sorties flown by OL-8 throughout 1968, 67 were operational missions; the remaining were Functional Check Flights (FCFs), or crew training/proficiency flights. As summer came to an end, OL-8's first three operational aircraft had each amassed close to 300 flying hours. In so doing they'd validated the concept of long-range, triple-sonic, high-altitude strategic reconnaissance within hostile airspace. It was now time for the first of many aircraft swap-outs to take place. Consequently, over seven days in September, Glowing Heat saw '980, '970 and '962 positioned to OL-8 from Beale, and '976, '974 and '978 returned home to undergo deep maintenance at the Lockheed Palmdale plant. Crew rotations were also an important part of OL-8s operating routine, and by the end of 1968, no fewer than 21 crews had flown the SR-71 into battle.

The SR-71 detachment at Kadena AB enjoyed excellent facilities inherited from the earlier CIA A-12 Oxcart program when it deployed to the island in 1967 during Operation *Black Shield*. (USAF via Tony Landis)

As the Vietnam War escalated, it also generated an increase in the demand for timely, high-quality reconnaissance imagery. This resulted in OL-8's SR-71 complement being increased in the spring 1970 changeover, from three to four aircraft (64-17969, '972, '973 and '974).

Having positioned 61-7976 from Beale AFB to Kadena on March 11, 1968, Majors Jerry O'Malley and his RSO Ed Payne flew the same aircraft on the SR-71's first ever operational mission ten days later. (USAF via Col Don Walbrecht)

The vast majority of Habu sorties during this period were in support of operations in Vietnam, but this wasn't exclusively the case. On the night of September 27, 1971, Majors Bob Spencer and "Butch" Sheffield got airborne from Okinawa in aircraft '980 and, having completed essential post-takeoff air refueling (AR), flew north. US Intelligence required details of the largest-ever Soviet naval exercise scheduled to take place in

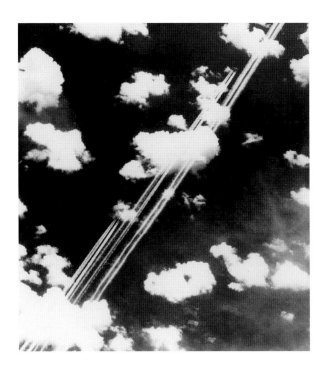

Captured during an operational mission over North Vietnam by an SR-71's Terrain Objective Camera (TROC), a cell of B-52s can be seen some 50,000ft below the Habu. (USAF)

the Sea of Japan, off the coast of the Soviet naval port of Vladivostok. The Habu was of course the ideal vehicle to "stimulate" the ELINT and COMINT environment of the Soviet fleet's defense systems. In addition, US national security officials were specifically interested in trying to obtain the latest signal characteristics of the Soviet's new SA-5 (Gammon) SAM system, deployed in defense of the important naval port. As '980 hurtled towards the target area, dozens of Soviet radars were switched on, but just short of entering Soviet airspace, the Habu was rolled into a full 35 degree banked turn, remaining throughout in international airspace – just.

On approach to the "collection area," however, Spencer noted that the right engine's oil pressure was dropping. When clear he discovered to his consternation that the reading had now fallen to zero and he was forced to shut the engine down, descend and decelerate to subsonic speed. But having stirred up a hornet's nest, the crew were now sitting ducks for any Soviet fast jets sent up to intercept the oil-starved Habu. Worse still, at much lower altitudes the SR-71 was subjected to strong head winds that rapidly depleted its fuel supply. Sheffield quickly calculated that their low-fuel state meant return to Okinawa was impossible – instead they'd have to divert to South Korea. But as they neared Korea, US listening posts reported the launch of several MiGs. In response, USAF F-102 Delta Dagger interceptors were scrambled from their base near Hon Chew, South Korea and vectored to position themselves between the MiGs and the Habu.

It was later established that the MiG launch was unconnected with the Habu's diversion, and recovery into Taegu was completed without further incident. When the EMR "take" was downloaded, it was found to have recorded emissions from no fewer than 290 different radar sites, but of greater importance was capture of the much sought-after SA-5 signal characteristics.

An hour before midnight on December 27, 1972, Giant Scale (the prefix given to all SR-71 operational sorties in the Pacific theater of operations) mission GS663, got underway with the launch of SR-71 '975. Flown by Col Darrell Cobb and his RSO Capt Reggie Blackwell in support of *Linebacker II* (an 11-day all-out assault on Hanoi using B-52s, calculated by the Nixon administration to bomb North Vietnamese politicians back to the Paris negotiating table), this proved to be the only Habu night sortie flown during the entire Vietnam War. Yet again the aircraft proved its worth, radiating a blinding ECM blanket in the target area to protect the lumbering B-52s against the SA-2 threat (only one Guam-based B-52 was lost on this raid). In addition the SR-71 secured a wealth of other intelligence data.

Yom Kippur

On April 26, 1971, Lt Cols Tom Estes and his RSO Dewain Vick established a stateside SR-71 endurance record after completing five full off-load air refuelings and staying aloft for five hours and 30 minutes. During that time they covered a distance of 15,000 miles and, in recognition of their achievement, were awarded the 1972 Harmon International Trophy. As it transpired, the sortie proved to be an extremely useful exercise for events that unraveled on the world stage just two years later.

On October 6, 1973, a meticulously planned attack, backed by the Soviet Union, was launched against Israel by Syria to the north and Egypt to the west. Two days before the assault began, the first in a series of Cosmos satellites was launched by the Soviets, which ensured that their Arab allies were provided with a steady stream of vital intelligence throughout the conflict. As Israeli soldiers prayed in their bunkers to mark Yom Kippur, five Egyptian infantry divisions supported by three mechanized and two armored divisions, were advancing along a 130-mile front within 15 minutes of the attack beginning. Ten pontoon bridges were thrown across the Suez Canal, the supposedly impregnable Bar-Lev Line was stormed, and bridgeheads were soon established on the East Bank. Simultaneously to the north, following a 30-minute artillery bombardment, a helicopter-borne commando attack, supported by three Syrian infantry divisions and two armored divisions, attacked the strategically important Golan Heights.

When Major Tony Bevacque and his RSO Major Jerry Crew returned to Kadena on July 26, 1968 from an operational mission in 61-7976 over North Vietnam, their TROC provided photographic confirmation that they were the first SR-71 crew members to have been fired upon by an SA-2 surface-to-air missile. History would subsequently prove this to be one of only two *confirmed* SA-2 firing incidents throughout the entire Senior Crown program. (USAF via Col Tony Bevacque)

The blitzkrieg-style attacks completely caught Western intelligence agencies off guard. To plug the intelligence void, CINCSAC General John Meyer ordered 9th SRW Commander, Col Pat Halloran, to prepare a series of SR-71 missions launched from the US eastern seaboard that would overfly the warring factions and recover into RAF Mildenhall, England. To that end Halloran hastily assembled a maintenance recovery team and, with them, embarked on a UK-bound KC-135Q tanker, with the intention of briefing senior Ministry of Defence (MoD) officials about the plan. However, upon arrival at Mildenhall, the team were dismayed to learn that, in a move calculated to ingratiate Arab approval and thereby hopefully secure the continued supply of Middle East oil, the Conservative government under Prime Minister Edward Heath had made a predictably futile decision to deny the UK's long-term ally operating authority from the UK base. So after only a few hours on the ground, Halloran and his team boarded another tanker and flew back to the US, recovering into Griffiss AFB, New York. In the meantime Lt Col Jim Shelton and his RSO Major Gary Coleman positioned SR-71 '979 to Griffiss. They were followed some hours later by Maj Al Joersz and Maj John Fuller in '964.

At 0200hrs on October 13, Shelton and Coleman got airborne in '979 and shortly afterwards completed the first air refueling hook-up in what was to be the SR-71's longest operational mission to date. Recovering back into Griffiss 10 hours 18 minutes later (six hours eight minutes of which was at Mach 3), the non-stop mission over the Middle East and back was supported by no

On June 26, 1982, Major Burnie Smith and his RSO Major Denny Whalen prepared to take 61-7980 on an operational mission to monitor North Korea. Also on the Kadena run-up area were Maj Lee Shelton and RSO Maj Russ Szczepanik in 61-7967, as they conducted checks prior to a Functional Check Flight (FCF). (USAF via Tony Landis)

fewer than 14 KC-135Q tankers – two from Griffiss, four from Goose Bay in Canada, and eight out of Torrejon AB, Spain.

The high-quality reconnaissance "take" provided intelligence and defense analysts with much needed information concerning the disposition of Arab forces in the region, which was in turn made available to the Israelis. In addition Congress granted President Richard Nixon his request for $2.2 billion in emergency aid for the Israelis, and the US began a huge airlift of war materials. This action incensed key Arab members of the Organization of Petroleum Exporting Countries (OPEC), who imposed a complete embargo on oil exports to the US, together with a unilateral 70 percent increase in oil prices and a five percent per month cut in production. The decision caused widespread panic in Western Europe, which depended on the Arab states for 80 percent of its oil.

By October 14, however, the situation on the Syrian front was swinging in favor of the Israelis. But in the Sinai desert the Egyptians launched a 100,000-strong offensive toward the east, and the result of this attack developed into one of the biggest tank battles in history. The Israeli forces gained ground and also established a bridgehead west of the Suez Canal that

On March 23, 1971, SR-71 pilot Major James Hudson was killed after his 'chute failed to fully deploy following ejection from an aborted takeoff in his T-38 (0-91606). The Instructor Pilot (IP), Lt Col Jack Thornton, in the front seat, stayed with the aircraft and suffered minor back injuries. Hudson would be the only Air Force SR-71 crew member to be killed during the entire Senior Crown program. (Appeal Democrat)

threatened to cut off the Egyptian army. With the Egyptian military situation becoming increasingly precarious, President Nixon announced that US forces across the globe had been placed on military alert following receipt of information indicating that the Soviet Union was planning "to send a very substantial force to the Middle East to relieve the beleaguered Egyptian Third Army, now completely encircled in the Sinai."

This tense period in superpower relations was somewhat defused when Soviet Secretary Brezhnev supported a United Nations motion of October 24 that would eventually end the Yom Kippur War. Meanwhile, however, SR-71 surveillance missions continued to monitor the situation.

Between October 13, 1973, and April 6, 1974, all nine of these long-distance missions launched from the US were successfully completed without a single ground or air abort (the final two sorties were flown from Seymour Johnson AFB, South Carolina, after the detachment moved south in order to escape the harsh New York winter). They represented the pinnacle of operational professionalism as well as bearing testament to the long reach of the aircraft and its ability to operate with impunity in a sophisticated, high-threat environment.

In September 1974, the first SR-71 (61-7972) visited the United Kingdom when it attended the Farnborough Air Display and established two transatlantic speed records that remain unbroken to this day. (USAF)

Records

Having already established a set of transatlantic records in 1974, the US bicentennial celebrations of 1976 provided the 9th SRW with an opportunity to break three more world absolute records. It was hoped that the attempts would be made on July 4, but due to administrative delays they were scheduled for July 27/28. Three crews and two aircraft (61-7958 and '962) were made ready for the attempts. Of the sorties flown on July 27, only one record could be verified, that of Speed Over a Closed Course of 1,000km, which was set by Majors Adolphus Bledsoe and his RSO John Fuller in '958 at 2,092mph.

Despite two aircraft having been made ready for the US bicentennial celebrations of 1976 (61-7958 and 61-7962), owing to weather and a maintenance issue, '958 was accorded the honor of gaining all three official absolute world speed and altitude records. A large white cross was applied to the underside of both aircraft to aid ground-based tracking cameras that monitored the flights. (USAF)

Cloud prevented the Nun Baker tracking cameras from recording the other flights throughout their entire course – a prerequisite insisted upon by the Fédération Aéronautique Internationale (FAI), the world governing body. So on July 28 Capt Robert Helt and his RSO Major Larry Elliott strapped into '962 to rerun their altitude attempt of the previous day. However, because of a maintenance issue, they switched into '958 and established an Altitude in Horizontal Flight record of 85,068ft. Aircraft '958 was used yet again, this time by Capt Eldon Joersz and his RSO Maj G. T. Morgan, and they carried off the Speed Over a Straight Course (15/25km) at 2,193mph.

North Korea

In addition to supporting in-theater operations during the Vietnam War, Det 1 were also tasked to provide Commander, United States Forces, Korea (COMUSK); Commander in Chief, Pacific Fleet (CINCPACFLT) and the Intelligence Center Pacific (ICPAC), with advanced warning of North Korean intentions by examining "indications and warning targets."

This region was designated a principal area of operations for two main considerations: that by 1977 North Korea had a standing army of 450,000 (making it the fifth largest in the world), and the unpredictability of the country's belligerent dictator – Kim Il Sung – who was committed to the reunification of the peninsula under his form of autocratic communism.

The North's propensity to relocate or reinforce its military units and installations along the Demilitarized Zone (DMZ) at night prompted US theater commanders to request that the majority of SR-71 sorties at this time be conducted at night. The JCS therefore directed SAC to increase the number of monthly SR-71 monitoring sorties to the area from eight to 12 per month. The SRC directed that the SR-71 be configured with cameras on the first two sorties and to thereafter gather Radar Intelligence (RADINT), using its HRR and ELINT, on the remaining ten missions. The Photo Intelligence (PHOTINT) provided a reference base for intelligence specialists to use when interpreting the HRR imagery.

So at 2105hrs on September 19, 1977, Maj Jack Veth and his RSO Maj Bill Keller departed Det 1 in SR-71 '960, returning 4.1hrs later, having completed the first night monitoring sortie of North Korea. Four additional RADINT/ELINT night sorties of North Korea were completed before the year's end.

The crews that flew these important missions were, however, less than impressed by their nocturnal forays, noting that the aircraft's cockpit lighting was uneven, causing reflections that made monitoring instrumentation extremely difficult and potentially dangerous – especially during the descent phase – to rendezvous with a tanker. Therefore, after the first two sorties the mission profile was amended, and the number of air refuelings reduced from two to one. The impact of this decision reduced the number of passes made through the sensitive area from two to one, which in turn also reduced the flight time from just under four and a half hours to approximately two and a half hours. In a further move to improve crew safety, subsequent missions were flown at Mach 2.8 and bank angles restricted to a maximum of 35 degrees (the situation was finally rectified in 1982, when cockpit lighting was improved and Peripheral Vision Horizon Display (PVHD) units were installed throughout the SR-71 fleet. These units projected a thin red line of light across the aircraft's instrument panel to produce an artificial horizon that responded to changes in aircraft pitch and roll, thereby duplicating the behavior of a natural horizon).

As is apparent, all SR-71 missions were highly regulated, but that didn't stop North Korea from voicing their disapproval of such flights. Matters came to a head on August 26, 1981, when '976 was fired upon by a North Korea SA-2 during the second, west to east, pass over the DMZ. The pilot, Maj Maury Rosenberg, saw the missile contrail and accelerated to Mach 3.2 whilst making a slight turn away from the SAM, which exploded a good 2 miles behind the Habu.

This extremely serious incident caused tensions on the peninsula to rise significantly. President Reagan roundly denounced "this act of lawlessness" – as usual, North Korea denied the missile firing charge, despite irrefutable photographic evidence to the contrary.

61-7979 launched from RAF Mildenhall on another operational mission. Note the shock-diamonds in the SR-71's exhaust plume and the various camouflage patterns applied to the C-130s in the background. (Paul F. Crickmore)

The first order of business after takeoff was to get a full fuel off-load from the trusty KC-135Q tanker. This ensured that there was no air remaining in the fuel tanks that could cause an explosion at cruise speed as a result of extreme thermodynamic heating – as the fuel depleted the void above it was filled with inert, gaseous nitrogen. (Lt Col Blair Bozek)

To help defuse the volatile situation, SR-71 reconnaissance flights to the area were suspended for six days, after which the reconnaissance line was moved even further to the south. On September 26, Deputy SECDEF Frank Carlucci visited Det 1, and explained that the DMZ route package had been moved further south only temporarily, and that the former routes would be reinstated after "certain preparations" were made – he didn't elaborate any further.

On October 3, Lt Gen Mathis (Assistant Vice Chief of Staff) held a special briefing for the Det's crew members, during which he outlined four special category missions which were to be flown on routes that replicated those flown during the August 26 shoot-down attempt. He emphasized that timings would be especially critical, and when questioned why by one of the pilots, the general explained that "Wild Weasel" anti-radar strike aircraft would be poised to hit any North Korean SAM site within 60 seconds of a launch against the SR-71. The tight time constraints would ensure that the strike aircraft were headed in the right direction at the moment a missile was launched. President Reagan had personally approved the plan.

On October 26, 1981, following extensive mission planning and detailed briefings, '975, flown by Maj B. C. Thomas and his RSO Maj Jay Reid, departed Kadena on the first of those four special missions. The mission was executed exactly as planned, and happily, for whatever reason, the North Koreans chose not to launch a missile at this or any other trawling mission, and all four sorties recovered safely after each four-hour flight.

Monitoring North Korea continued to be a key mission for Det 1's SR-71s; indeed, the final operational sortie flown from Kadena before Senior Crown was deactivated was a 3.4 hour flight, flown in the vicinity by SR-71 '962 on September 25, 1989, by Maj Don Watkins and his RSO Maj Bob Fowlkes.

 SA-2 OVER THE DMZ

On August 26, 1981, an incident occurred that could have sparked a political crisis of unimaginable proportions. Majors Maury Rosenberg and his RSO ED McKim were flying SR-71 61-7976 at Mach 3 and 77,000ft on a routine reconnaissance mission over the DMZ between North and South Korea, when the North fired an SA-2 at them. Maury saw the missile contrail, turned slightly left and increased speed to Mach 3.2; as a result, luckily the missile missed.

The Iran–Iraq War

On September 24, 1980, a simmering border war between Iraq and Iran flared into a ten-year-long war of attrition. Both the USSR and the US made it clear that they would remain strictly neutral. However, the US intelligence community understood how Iran could easily exploit the oil pressure point, particularly as oil-laden tankers passed through a natural choke point at the Straits of Hormuz.

As the situation in the Gulf continued to escalate, Giant Express – SAC's codename for SR-71 operational sorties around the Indian Ocean – was initiated when the first of four extremely long, non-stop reconnaissance missions to the area was completed by Majors Mike Smith and Doug Soifer from Kadena on July 22, 1987, in '967. These 11-hour sorties involved two air refuelings on the outbound leg and three on the return. The most distant second and third tankings were conducted by three KC-10s that were able to extend their range by "buddy" refueling each other. All four missions were judged to be extremely successful, revealing the presence of Iranian Silkworm surface-to-surface missiles and masses of other military equipment in the Gulf. Thus intelligence services were able to forewarn the US Navy of the Silkworm threat, and diplomats were able to bring pressure to bear on Iran. Yet again the SR-71 had performed a vital strategic intelligence-gathering mission in a distant part of the world.

Det 4 operations

Giant Reach was SAC's codename for SR-71 European operations. The plan originally envisaged operating the SR-71 on a 30-day Temporary Duty (TDY) basis from Torrejon Air Base, Spain. However, Spanish law prohibited such flights, so the plan was modified, and instead, home for such operations would be RAF Mildenhall, England.

As noted earlier, the first operational requirement to implement Giant Reach occurred on October 6, 1973, following the outbreak of the Yom Kippur War. However, as the UK government had banned such flights, the first Habu to visit England was aircraft 61-7972, on September 1, 1974. The purpose of the flight was to participate in the static display at the world-renowned Farnborough air show. During the positioning flight, a new transatlantic speed record was established from New York to London of just 1 hour 54 minutes – a record that stands to this day. Having been top of the bill at Farnborough, another crew returned the aircraft to Beale AFB, on September 13, establishing in the process yet another world speed record, this time from London to Los Angeles in 3 hours 47 minutes.

Detailed route planning for Mildenhall sorties was conducted at the SRC. Details of the proposed tracks were then sent to the 98th Strategic Wing, at Torrejon AB, as this unit was responsible for SAC operations from Mildenhall at the time. Detachment 1 of the 98th SW then coordinated all necessary prior clearances with appropriate British officials. On April 20, 1976, SR-71 '972 again visited the UK, accompanied by two KC-135Q support tankers – but this visit was strictly business. Two missions were flown in an attempt to gather HRR imagery of the five important naval bases located in the Barents Sea, at Zapadnya, Litsa, Vidyayevo, Gadzhievo, Severomorsk and Gremikha – home of the Soviet Union's powerful Northern Fleet. But off the west coast of Norway the aircraft encountered unseasonably high outside air temperatures, resulting in a disproportionately high fuel burn. The Habu would barely be able to reach its tankers, so the crew prudently aborted the mission and returned to Mildenhall. Although the sortie failed to complete the reconnaissance-gathering phase of the mission, it did obtain extremely useful information that helped shape the aircraft's flight profile and operating procedures when flying in the confined and often challenging conditions of Northern Europe.

Two large NATO training exercises were scheduled in the autumn of 1976, and Headquarters European Command were keen that the SR-71 should participate in both. As a result 61-7962 arrived on September 6, 1976. Six sorties

An SR-71 working in conjunction with an RC-135V "Rivet Joint" aircraft made for a good ELINT gathering team. The Habu was guaranteed to stimulate the electronic environment, as radar operators switched their sets on to track the high-speed, high-flying "target." Meanwhile, standing off 20–30 miles beyond, the RC would use its banks of receivers to "hoover up" and triangulate the signals, thereby establishing the potential enemy's Electronic Order of Battle (EOB). (USAF)

were flown and both types of HRR imagery, PHOTINT and ELINT, were collected of Soviet/Warsaw Pact positions in East Germany, as well as the Soviet sub pens as attempted by '972 earlier in the year. The aircraft returned to Beale after a highly successful European tour that lasted 19 days.

Following a significant restructure, the 98th SW was deactivated on December 31, 1976, and command transferred to the 306th SW. It was also decided that the 306th SW's commander would report directly to the CINCSAC, who accorded him "delegated authority" to exercise command responsibilities for all present and future SAC European operations – these included the European Tanker Force, RC-135 TDY deployments, as well as any future B-52 or U-2R/SR-71 deployments.

This increase in SAC's European presence was in direct response to a significant increase in the nature of the Soviet/Warsaw Pact threat facing NATO. SAC wanted to deploy B-52s and tankers periodically to England in order to train crews to a level that made them capable of performing a wartime tactical mission. The U-2R and SR-71 would be required to provide complementary prestrike and bomb damage assessment (BDA) imagery, in addition to Signals Intelligence (SIGINT). Therefore, as far as the Commander in Chief USAFE was concerned, it was "most desirous" that the SR-71 and U-2R deploy regularly to RAF Mildenhall to monitor the situation.

On January 17, 1977, a third ten-day SR-71 deployment was completed by 61-7958, and in February Headquarters SAC proposed to the JCS that they seek approval for a 17-day deployment to Mildenhall, during which time one training sortie and two Peacetime Aerial Reconnaissance Program (PARPRO) missions were to be flown. They further requested that both of the PARPRO missions be approved to collect ELINT and HRR imagery, as they were anxious to demonstrate the unique characteristics of the latter to other potential national intelligence users – the US Army and US Navy. The JCS duly issued SAC with the necessary authorization to proceed and furthermore went on to direct Headquarters SAC to deploy to Mildenhall a Mobile Processing Center (MPC), held in storage at Beale.

The MPC consisted of 24 trailer-like vans and collectively contained all the equipment necessary to process raw intelligence data collected by the SR-71's HRR and cameras in theater. The entire package was transported to the UK in

Prior to penetrating the Barents Sea, during an operational mission on October 6, 1981, 61-7964, call sign MINTY 23, flown by Major Rich Judson and RSO Lt Col Frank Kelly, clears the tanker after completing a full fuel disconnect in the Viking North refueling area off the coast of Bodo, Norway. (Paul F. Crickmore)

two C-5s and four C-141s. On arrival the complex was located inside a hangar and within a secure compound, and it was operational when SR-71, 61-7958, touched down at the UK base on May 16, 1977.

Satisfactorily completing the training sortie over the North Sea on May 18, the first PARPRO mission of an SR-71 from the UK was successfully completed two days later. Yet again the collection area was Murmansk, but unlike previous sorties, this mission was coordinated with an RC-135V Rivet Joint. However, during the mission planning stage it was discovered that the Soviets had issued a NOTAM (Notice To Airman), warning of surface-to-air missile test firing to altitudes in excess of 100,000ft, and it happened to be located exactly at the point where the SR-71 was planned to ingress and egress the Barents Sea: had the mission been compromised? Despite some misgivings, the mission went ahead and proved an outstanding success, capturing not only some outstanding HRR imagery of subs in their pens, but the ELINT systems carried by both aircraft also recorded the first ever RF signals associated with a particular SA-5 variant.

Yemen

In early 1979, another threat of war seemed to be looming in the Middle East, this time between North and South Yemen, which borders oil-rich Saudi Arabia – one of the largest suppliers of oil to the West.

In response to a Saudi request made through the Defense Intelligence Agency (DIA), the JCS directed HQ SAC to deploy an SR-71 to Mildenhall on March 12, 1979 – tasked to conduct a Giant Reach special mission into the Middle East and secure surveillance relating to events that had developed in this latest hot-spot. Following two early morning runway aborts caused by bad weather in Yemen, the mission finally got underway at 0430hrs on March 16. As the French refused permission for the SR-71 to overfly their airspace, it was necessary for 61-7972 to route around the Iberian peninsula to access the Mediterranean. This added considerably to both mission endurance time and the number of KC-135Q support tankers; however, after over nine hours in their pressure suits, the crew recovered '972 safely back at their temporary Suffolk home. The mission was a complete success, having acquired all the intelligence data required by the National Security Council (NSC), and on March 28 the Habu was repositioned back to Beale.

Such was the proven success of the SR-71 in the European Theater of Operations (ETO) that on March 31, 1979, Detachment 4 of the 9 SRW was established at Mildenhall – at this time, a joint unit operating both the SR-71 and TR-1.

On December 12 the third SR-71 deployment in 1980 was made to Mildenhall. This time the JCS directed that the deployment should take place in response to a request from the Commander in Chief Atlantic (CINCATL), who was concerned at the possible intervention of Soviet military forces to quell rising dissent in Poland. Aircraft 61-7964 duly arrived at Mildenhall, having collected HRR/ELINT off the Baltic coast on its inbound leg to Mildenhall. This was to prove a milestone deployment, as the aircraft stayed in the UK for four months. On March 6, the day before its return to Beale, it was replaced by 61-7972, which in turn stayed for two months before eventually departing on May 5, 1981.

During a Barents/Baltic mission on June 29, 1987, in aircraft 61-7964, Maj Duane Noll and his RSO Maj Tom Veltri experienced an explosion in the aircraft's right engine whilst off the coasts of Communist-controlled Lithuania, Latvia and Estonia. Major Noll handled the emergency with exceptional skill and diverted safely into Nordholz AB, West Germany. This photo was taken by the pilot of a Swedish Air Force Saab 37 Viggen that helped escort the damaged aircraft – note the wide-open position of the aircraft's right exhaust feathers. (Swedish Air Force)

Ten days after Operation *El Dorado Canyon*, the raid against Col Gadaffi's Libya, 61-7980 was still equipped with its "glass-nose," within which was situated the OBC. (Bob Archer)

One round-robin flight from Beale to the Barents Sea and back was scheduled on August 12, 1981. However, having cleared the target area and hooked up to a tanker, '964's oil warning light illuminated continuously. This required the crew to divert to the closest base from their current position, which turned out to be Bodo in Norway – this was the first occasion that an SR-71 landed in continental Europe. Having notified the SRC of their intentions to divert, the crew later communicated the nature of the problem to Mildenhall, and a KC-135Q with a maintenance team on board was duly dispatched. Finally, on August 16, the SR-71 recovered into Mildenhall. Now christened on its twin tails "The Bodonian Express," '964 continued flying operational sorties from Mildenhall until November 6, when it was returned to Beale.

Throughout the turmoil and political unrest in Poland toward the end of 1981, SR-71s flown from Mildenhall helped provide the US national leadership with regularly updated intelligence reports regarding possible Soviet intervention, by utilizing its HRR and ELINT sensors to monitor the situation. This was achieved by adhering rigidly to a PARPRO route flown anti-clockwise around the Baltic Sea, in international airspace.

Despite the 1983 deployment to Mildenhall still being referred to as a temporary operation, two SR-71s remained at the base for virtually the entire year. But following meetings between officials from the USAF and Ministry of Defence (MoD), these arrangements changed on April 5, 1984, when Prime Minister Thatcher announced that a permanent detachment of SR-71 aircraft had been formed at the Suffolk base.

The resurgence of Islamic fundamentalism in the Middle East in the early 1980s and the general destabilizing effect that this had throughout the region guaranteed that the SR-71 would be kept busy monitoring many of these hotspots. Missions over the Lebanon were flown by Det 4 crews to keep tabs on the Syrian and Israeli armies, as well as on various contraband movements that supplied Islamic Jihad warriors and other supporting groups. However, after confrontations in the Gulf of Sidra, and various terrorist activities, it was Libya that proved to be the next major flashpoint.

Following meticulous planning, Operation *El Dorado Canyon* was a combined strike by US Navy and USAF assets against specific Libyan military targets identified around Tripoli and Benghazi. The attack was launched during the small hours of April 15, 1986. The acquisition of aerial reconnaissance photographs to enable photo interpreters (PIs) to complete BDA reports was an essential task demanded by the Supreme Commander himself – President Reagan. However, with the sophisticated, integrated Libyan air defense system on full alert immediately after the raid, it was the SR-71 that possessed the necessary performance and systems capability that could survive in such a high-risk environment and acquire the quality imagery demanded by the PIs.

On consecutive days, a total of three missions were flown by Det 4 crews over the strike areas. The French, as usual, refused overflight access into the Mediterranean, necessitating a laborious flight around the Iberian Peninsula and entry via the Straits of Gibraltar, adding significantly to the flight time. The importance of these SR-71 missions required the use of an airborne spare, to cover possible mechanical malfunctions in the primary aircraft. The first of these high-profile sorties was completed in 61-7980. Unfortunately, cloud cover over Tripoli prevented any useful imagery from this area being collected by the aircraft's cameras. Use of the SR-71's HRR would have easily solved this problem. However, senior officials at the Pentagon wanted to release imagery to the world's media to prove that the attacks were proportionate, selective and accurate, but the highly classified nature of the SR-71's HRR capabilities prevented this. Consequently, a second mission was completed in 61-7960, but the aircraft suffered a sensor failure, so a third sortie was flown on April 17, again in aircraft '980. This series of sorties proved unparalleled in over 20 years of SR-71 operations. Six missions had been flown in three days by just two aircraft, supported by a maintenance team that was staffed to support only two to three sorties a week.

THE LONG FAREWELL

Two operating issues plagued the Senior Crown program for most of its life, namely its high operating costs in comparison to other fixed-wing assets, and provision to fund those costs. Initially, the cost versus benefit argument was straightforward to justify (particularly during the Vietnam War), on the basis that the detailed, broad synoptic coverage secured by the platform was essential for both national and theater commanders, and that the acquisition of such material was beyond the capability of other platforms to secure – especially in high-threat environments.

Senior Crown's Program Element number at the Pentagon was PE 11133F (the first digit, 1, denoted the major force program as strategic). Initially DOD funding for this was provisioned for under a special category called the "black world." This protected from scrutiny funds for highly classified programs and also stabilized funding levels from cyclical budgetary raids that were the bane of "white world" programs. Transfer of the management of Senior Crown from

Lt Cols Tom McCleary (right) and his RSO Stan Gudmondson say their farewells to various Tech Reps and the Crew Chief before departing the UK for the last time on January 18, 1990. (Paul F. Crickmore)

the Air Staff Programs division to the Air Staff Operations division (XOORS) occurred shortly before August 1969. Then, in 1975, XXORS was redesignated XOORZ and SR-71 funding was also moved from the black into the white world. From then on Senior Crown had to compete for its funding against all other DOD programs. This situation provided the SR-71's Program Element Monitor (PEM) at XOORZ with two problems. The classified nature of the program meant that it was designated Top Secret/Sensitive Compartmented Information (TS/SCI), which in practical terms meant that only those with specific clearances and a need-to-know were party to the intelligence it generated, which inevitably corseted the level of support the PEM could muster. The second problem was that the first digit in the program element number, identifying Senior Crown as "strategic," meant that it fell under the command of SAC, whose primary responsibility was to secure funding for two of the three legs of the nuclear triad – nuclear intercontinental ballistic missiles and its force of nuclear equipped B-52 bombers (a budgetary situation further exacerbated by the need to upgrade both systems and introduce the B-1 bomber). Therefore, to some extent SAC's later anti-SR-71 stance is understandable, since they were saddled with its entire operating costs while other government agencies, including the US Navy and US Army who were major beneficiaries of its reconnaissance, contributed nothing to its upkeep.

One of the vagaries of change in any large organization, especially at the top, is that the incumbent has his/her own agenda. When ex-SR-71 pilot (later to become 9th SRW Commander, and ultimately Commander of Tactical Air Command), Gen Jerry O'Malley, was tragically killed in a freak accident on

E MiG INTERCEPTION

During a reconnaissance mission into the Barents Sea "collection area" on October 6, 1986, aircraft 61-7980 was crewed by Majors Ed Yeilding and his RSO Curt Osterheld. Whilst in a left banked turn, Ed spotted an aircraft that subsequently turned out to be a MiG-31 "Foxhound," flown by Maj Mikhail Myagkiy of the 174th GvIAP, sent up on a practice interception against them.

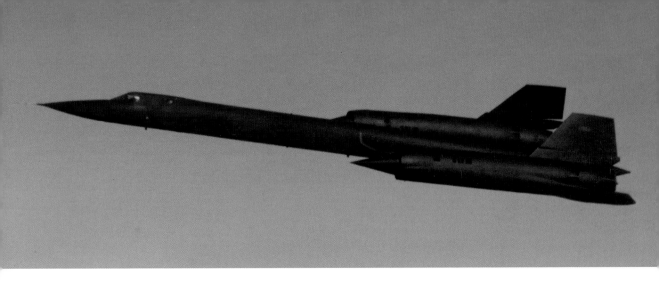

After Senior Crown was terminated on November 22, 1989, a minimum number of crew proficiency flights were made before aircraft from the Dets were positioned back to the states. Aircraft 61-7962 was ferried back from Kadena on January 21, 1990. At Mildenhall, 61-7967 was ferried back on January 19; but having completed a couple of memorable passes for the press the day before, McCleary and Gudmondson then proceeded on an operational sortie into the Barents Sea before returning to Beale – a stylish way of also bidding farewell to their old adversary. (Paul F. Crickmore)

April 20, 1985, the USAF lost a top leader tipped to become the Air Force's next Chief of Staff. Senior Crown also lost one of its most powerful supporters. The SR-71 didn't feature in the non-O'Malley Air Force. The platform was living on borrowed time without an electro-optical system for its cameras and without its Advanced Synthetic Aperture Radar System (ASARS), connected to a data link, to enable real-time/near real-time transmission of its reconnaissance data. Unequivocally the program's main detractor was Chief of Staff General Larry Welch, but other prominent/ influential figures included General Dugan, AF/XO; General John Chain, CINCSAC; General Ron Fogleman, AF/Program Requirements; General Doyle, Chief of SAC Intelligence (SAC/IN); Col Tanner, also of SAC/IN; and General Leo Smith of the Budget Review Board. Their assault on Senior Crown began from mid-1986 and the main reasons that they cited for retiring the SR-71 was cost and marginal benefits over satellites. By 1988 it looked as though their efforts would be successful. However, Admiral Lee Baggot, CINCLANT, insisted that no other platforms (including satellites), were capable of gathering the vital intelligence he required regarding the Soviet subs based on the Kola Peninsula. He took his battle right to the JCS and managed to secure funding for Det 4 for a further year. In addition, the extremely resourceful SR-71 PEM at XOORZ managed to obtain funding from a staffer serving on the Senate Appropriations Committee that enabled the SR-71 logistics facility at Palmdale and Det 1 to remain open for fiscal year (FY) '89. But as the end of that fiscal approached, the future of the program looked increasingly bleak, and on October 1, 1989, all SR-71 operations were suspended, with the exception of a minimum number of proficiency flights. Finally, on November 22, despite the misgivings of 40 members of Congress, including Senator Sam Nunn, chairman of the Senate Committee on Armed Services, Senior Crown was terminated. Two months later, on January 26, 1990, the SR-71 was officially decommissioned in a ceremony at Beale AFB – the program's detractors had finally won the day.

On August 2, 1990, Iraq invaded Kuwait and within days of the invasion Ben Rich (now President of the Skunk Works), phoned General Michael Loh, Air Force Vice Chief of Staff, and informed him that he could have three SR-71s ready for operations over the Gulf within 90 days. General Loh committed to float the idea and get back. But about a week later, Rich received a call saying that SecDef, Dick Cheney vetoed the idea, commenting along the lines, "I retired that airplane once, I'm not going to do it again. If

I bring it back now, I'll never get rid of it." That *Desert Storm*, the subsequent Allied operation that ousted Saddam Hussein's forces from Kuwait, was a spectacular success, is beyond question. However, one of the lessons learned from the 41-day campaign was that there was a lack of timely reconnaissance material available to General Schwarzkopf's field commanders – a gap that could have been bridged by the SR-71.

In compliance with the decommission decision, three SR-71s were placed in storage at Air Force Site 2, Palmdale. But virtually all other remaining aircraft – including the surviving A-12 Oxcarts, were cut up, moved and reconstructed as exhibits at various museums around the United States. However, as noted earlier, NASA required the use of three aircraft as supersonic test platforms to be flown from Edwards AFB.

Further discontent about the decision to terminate Senior Crown reemerged during the spring of 1994, when relations between North Korea and the United States sank to another low over North Korea's refusal to allow inspection of their nuclear sites. This action prompted Senator Robert Byrd and several members of Congress to contend that, back in 1990, the Pentagon had consistently lied about the supposed readiness of an SR-71 replacement. Their campaigning paid dividends, as noted in the Department of Defense Appropriation Bill 1995, dated July 20, when $100,000,000 was made available for the reactivation of a modest (three plane) SR-71 Blackbird reconnaissance aircraft contingent for intelligence operations, as recommended by the Senate Armed Services Committee. Furthermore, in an unprecedented move, their report went on to detail how and where the money was to be spent during that first year – including co-locating the new detachment at Edwards AFB in order to share some operating facilities with NASA, thereby helping to reduce costs, as well as implementing a robust sensor update program.

When the "anti-SR-71 lobby" based within the Pentagon managed to kill the Senior Crown program on November 22, 1989, Lockheed photographer Eric Schulzinger composed and took this historic photograph at Beale AFB. (Lockheed Martin)

Recognizing the utility of the aircraft's systems to both national and tactical intelligence commanders, the Committee also directed that costs should be evenly shared by the intelligence community and the Tactical Intelligence and Related Activities (TIARA) budget. The conferees went on to reaffirm their support for the goals and objectives of the department's endurance unmanned aerial vehicle program, and further directed that the SR-71 program be wholly designated as a TIARA program and that the Air Force assume total responsibility for sustaining out-year budget requirements.

The scale and detail of this Congressionally Directed Action, or CDA, is astonishing, and no doubt acted as a red rag to a bull to those senior Air Force officers that had worked so tirelessly to terminate Senior Crown. In a memo dated October 24, 1994, to the Deputy Chief of Staff, Plans and Operations USAF, from the Director, DARO, Major General Kenneth R. Israel, the latter pointedly recognized, "Currently, no funding has been identified for FY1996 and out."

Aircraft reactivation began on January 5, 1995. Of the three platforms placed in deep storage at Palmdale, only 61-7967 was called to arms by the Air Force. The other A model to be recommissioned was 61-7971, which was one of the three aircraft to have been loaned to NASA. Three months after the reactivation date, '971 had undertaken all the necessary equipment installs and, following a second FCF, was signed-off mission-ready. In contrast it took seven FCFs to wring out all glitches in '967, which wasn't declared ready to join the line until January 12, 1996.

Three Air Force crews were checked out utilizing the SR-71B. To keep flight hours low and thereby save money, two crews were maintained at Mission Ready flight status, with the third crew designated Mission Capable. But the CDA had created an immense amount of resentment amongst several members of Congress and key AF officers, including none other than the now USAF Chief of Staff, General Fogleman. Det 2 was operationally ready to deploy, but they were never tasked to do so by the Air Force. Basically, senior AF figures were planning for a 12-month, womb to tomb scenario, believing that Congress would be unable to push through additional funding for a second year. However, against the odds, $35 million of further funds were appropriated for the SR-71, as noted in the National Defense Authorization Act for FY 1996: "The committee is pleased with the timely and cost-effective reconstitution of a contingency force manned, high speed, penetrating reconnaissance aircraft as a hedge until penetrating unmanned aerial vehicles are more widely fielded."

Despite monies being appropriated, significantly, there was no mention of it in the Senate Authorization Bill. Furthermore, when a staffer on the House Select Committee on Intelligence pointed out that Section 504 of the 1947 National Security Act actually prohibits the obligation of funds for intelligence activities not specifically authorized, this was taken up in a meeting of Congress in December 1995. The Air Staff were left to debate where this technicality left the SR-71, given that the budget was split between two pots of money – Aircraft Procurement and Operation & Maintenance. With conflicting guidance coming from Congress on how Section 504 should be interpreted, lawyers became involved, after which it was determined that in order to comply with the letter of the law, SR-71 operations had to be suspended. A signal was therefore dispatched to that effect at 23:00 Z (the military term for GMT) on April 16, 1996, and all Air Force SR-71 flying ceased yet again.

Whilst grounded, two classified requests were made for SR-71 operations,

but both were denied based upon the interpretation of intelligence laws. But with members of the Senate Appropriations Committee enraged at the way they'd been circumvented over the decision to suspend SR-71 operations, they made it known that if their bid to secure $30 million worth of funding for the SR-71 was obstructed, they threatened to have Section 8080 of the Appropriations Act eliminated. After which, their next tactic would have been to get the Intelligence Authorization Act for FY97 defeated on the House and Senate floors, which in turn would have led to the suspension of *all* intelligence activities. Perhaps not surprisingly, the bill was passed and flying resumed once more. However, by now the powers that be in the Air Force had had enough of "unwanted intervention" by Congress in their affairs, and when the White House insisted that the Pentagon find savings in the defense budget, senior AF officers seized their opportunity and offered up the SR-71. On October 14, 1997, President Bill Clinton line-item vetoed the program and with immediate effect all Air Force Blackbird flying ceased – this time permanently.

In yet another twist later that year, the US Supreme Court ruled that the line-item veto was unconstitutional. Two other programs that fell victim to this veto process were reinstated by the Air Force – not, however, the SR-71. Yet again, elements within Congress stood their ground, stating that funds totalling $39 million were available for the program and demanded to know the source of the holdup. But when required, the bureaucratic process can be made to slow to a snail's pace, and by stalling, on October 1, 1998 (the start of FY 1999), whatever funding that had remained was exhausted. The SR-71 wasn't in the budget and it was all over, this time for good.

Aircraft 61-7967 is seen sporting markings applied during the brief SR-71 reactivation that occurred as a consequence of the September 1994 Congressionally Directed Action (CDA). (USAF)

Throughout all the political shenanigans during the reactivation of Det 2, the SR-71 had flown a total of 150 training sorties during 365.7 flight hours. The final Det 2, SR-71 sortie was flown on October 10, 1997, in aircraft '967 on training route Brandy, which lasted 4.1 hours.

CONCLUSION

As an aeronautical accomplishment, the Lockheed SR-71 and its immediate predecessor the A-12 Oxcart, stand without peer. They remain the fastest, highest flying operational aircraft ever to see service. Of equal importance from an operational perspective is the fact that their designs were also the first to employ stealth techniques and technologies to generate a minimal RCS return, thereby greatly reducing their chances of interception. Considering all these factors, it is perhaps even more remarkable that they were designed at a time when computers were in their infancy, and to a large extent the highly complex mathematical equations behind these amazingly complex masterpieces were solved using slide-rules.

The SR-71 first flew just two years after the Cuban Missile Crisis – a time when both Cold War superpowers stared nuclear Armageddon squarely in the face. Today, more than five decades later, it's perhaps difficult to grasp how very real were the preparations to implement the policy of so-called Mutually Assured Destruction (MAD), but the SR-71's war role evolved during this era and it was very much a part of the nuclear Single Integrated Operational Plan (SIOP).

After the Vietnam and Yom Kippur wars, Senior Crown continued to play a central part in monitoring, from just within international airspace, the activities of the Soviet Union/WarPac and Communist China through the Peacetime Aerial Reconnaissance Program (PARPRO). Therefore, unlike its CIA predecessor the A-12, the USAF-operated SR-71 had a full and legitimate role to play in an ever-changing world.

Satellite capabilities continued to improve during the 20-plus years of operational life of Senior Crown, and inevitably this impacted upon the SR-71's role. But a sophisticated, manned aircraft, gathering timely, synoptic reconnaissance over high-threat battlefields remains a true force multiplier.

Since the end of the Cold War and the termination of the SR-71 program, there have been many scenarios in war zones in which the US has become involved where field commanders have struggled for the want of better intelligence. This "intelligence gap" could, on many occasions, have been bridged by an SR-71 equipped with the upgraded real-time/near-real-time sensors with which Det 2's aircraft were equipped in 1997. It's interesting to speculate whether the SR-71 program would have enjoyed a more prolonged career had it been allocated to the intelligence budget, rather than SAC's.

There can be little doubt that the mix of reconnaissance data gathered by satellites and the latest generation of highly sophisticated/capable UAVs is serving the US intelligence community extremely well. What isn't quite as clear is whether the historical decision made, primarily by senior Air Force officers, to retire Senior Crown as early as they did was subsequently proven to be ill-advised.

BIBLIOGRAPHY

Byrnes, Donn A. and Hurley, Kenneth D., *Blackbird Rising: Birth of an Aviation Legend*, Saga Mesa Publications (1999)

Crickmore, Paul F., *Lockheed A-12 The CIA's Blackbird and other variants*, Osprey, Oxford (2014)

Crickmore, Paul F., *Lockheed Blackbird Beyond the Secret Missions*, Osprey, Oxford (1993 – revised 2010)

Crickmore, Paul F., *Lockheed SR-71 Operations in Europe and the Middle East*, Osprey, Oxford (2009)

Crickmore, Paul F., *Lockheed SR-71 Operations in the Far East*, Osprey, Oxford (2008)

Davies, Steve and Crickmore, Paul F., *Lockheed SR-71 Blackbird Owners' Workshop Manual*, Haynes Publishing, Yeovil (2012)

Graham, Col. Richard H., *Flying the SR-71 Blackbird in the Cockpit on a Secret Operational Mission*, Zenith Press, (2008)

Graham, Col. Richard H., *SR-71 Blackbird Stories, Tales, and Legends*, MBI (2002)

Graham, Col. Richard H. *SR-71 Revealed The Inside Story*, MBI (1996)

Graham, Col. Richard H. *SR-71 The Complete Illustrated History of The Blackbird, The World's Highest, Fastest Plane*, Zenith Press (2013)

Goodall, James and Miller, Jay, *Lockheed's SR-71 'Blackbird' Family A-12, F-12, M21, D21,SR-71*, Aerofax Inc., Tulsa (2002)

Johnson, Clarence L. "Kelly" and Smith, Maggie, *More than my share of it all*, Smithsonian, Washington (1985)

Landis, Tony R., *Lockheed Blackbird Family A-12, YF-12, D-21/M-21 & SR-71 Photo Scrapbook*, Specialty Press, North Branch (2010)

Lovick Jr, Edward, *Radar Man: A Personal History of Stealth*, iUniverse, Bloomington (2010)

Merlin, Peter W., *From Archangel to Senior Crown: Design and Development of the Blackbird*, American Institute of Aeronautics and Astronautics, Reston (2008)

Miller, Jay, *Lockheed's Skunk Works: The first fifty years*, Aerofax, Inc.,Tulsa (1993)

Rich, Ben R. and Janos, Leo, *Skunk Works*, Little, Brown, Boston (1994)

Stanley II, Col. Roy M., *Asia From Above: The 67th Reconnaissance Technical Squadron, Yokota AB, Japan, July 1957 to March 1971*, Author House, Bloomington (2006)

Documents

SR-71A Flight Manual, Secretary of the Air Force (1986)

INDEX

Note: Page references in **bold** refer to photographs and/or captions. References in brackets refer to plate captions.

1947 National Security Act 60
1964 presidential election campaign 7–8
1995 Department of Defense Appropriation Bill 59

ADS (Accessory Drive System) 26, 28
AICS (Air Inlet Control System) 26–27, **27**
air refuelling 17, 40, 41, 43, 47, **48**, 50
aircraft: Boeing B-52 bomber 51, 56; Boeing KC-135 aerial refuelling aircraft 17, 40, 43, 44, **48**, 50, 53, 54; Boeing RC-135 Rivet Joint reconnaissance aircraft **51**, 52; F-104 Starfighter interceptor fighter 4, **9**; Lockheed A-12 reconnaissance aircraft 4, 5, **5**, 9, 10, 59; MiG-31 "Foxhound" interceptor (USSR) **E57(56)**; North American XB-70 bomber 6, **6**, 8; U-2 reconnaissance aircraft 4, 10
airframe construction **22**, 22–23, **23**
altitudes 4, 23, **25**, 27, 37
ANS (Astro-Inertial Navigation System) 5–6, 14, 30, 32, 34
ASARS II (Advanced Synthetic Aperture Radar System) **18**, 32–33, 58

Barents Sea missions 50, 52, **52**, **53**, 54, **E57(56)**
battery supply 28
Beale AFB 12, 14, 38–39, 40, 41, 50, 51, 53–54, **59**
"Black World" aviation program 5, 7–8, 55
bleed bypass system 24–25, 27
bombing of Libya **54**, 55
budgets and cost constraints **6**, 7, 9, 55–56, 59–61

cameras 10, **19**, **30**, 32–34, **33**, **34**, 40, **42**, **43**, 46, **46**
CAPRE (Capability Reconnaissance Radar) 32
CIA, the 4, **5**, 9, 34
CITs (Compressor Inlet Temperatures) 24–25
classified data 34, 36, 39, 55–56, 60–61
CMDIs (Color Multifunctional Display Indicators) **29**
cockpits **29**, 47
COMINT 42
constitutionality of a presidential line-item veto 61
contract for radar system 5

DAFICS (Digital Automatic Flight and Inlet Control System) 27, 29–30
DEF (Defensive Electronic Systems) **35**, 35–36
design and development 4, 5–7, 14, **19**, 62
dichotomy between cameras and synoptic coverage 10

ECM (Electronic Counter Measures) **19**, **35**, 35–36
EGT (Exhaust Gas Temperature) 25
electrical power 28
elevons 29
ELINT (Electronic Intelligence) 10, 34, 42, 46, 51, **51**, 52, 54
EMR (Electromagnetic Reconnaissance System) 34, 42
endurance record 42–43
engine power 24–27, **25**, **26**, **27**

Farnborough air show **45**, 50
federal funding issues 59–61
First Gulf War, the 58–59
flight controls **29**, 29–30
FMC (Forward Motion Compensation) 32, 33, 34
fuel and ignition system 23–24, **25**, **26**
funding of highly classified programs 56–57

gas effects of an aerospike engine 20
generator problems 41
Giant Reach operations 50–52, 53

Gilliland, Robert J. 8–9, **9**, **A10**, **10**
ground-mapping 33

Harmon International Trophy, the 43
HRR imagery 50–51, 52, 54, 55
hydraulic systems 24, 25, 26, 28, 29

inaugural flight **9**, **10**, 40, 41
incursions into Soviet airspace 9–10, 50, 52, **52**, **53**, 54, **E57(56)**
inlet spikes 22, 26, 28
"intelligence gap" since retirement of the SR-71 62
Iran-Iraq War, the 50

jammer systems **35**, 35–37
JCS (Joint Chiefs of Staff) 7, 39, 46, 51, 53, 58
Johnson, Clarence L. "Kelly" 4, 5, **6**, 6–7, 8, 13
Johnson, Lyndon B. 7–8, 9, 38
JP-7 fuel 24

Kirchhoff's law of thermal radiation 22

LASRE (Linear Aerospike SR-71 Experiment) project **19**, 20, **C21(20)**
legacy of the SR-71 62
liquid nitrogen 24
Lockheed SR-71: SR-71A **40**; 61-7951 **A11(10)**, 19; 61-7953 16, **17**; 61-7955 **A11(10)**, 18, **18**; 61-7959 **A11(10)**, 52; 61-7962 **D31(30)**, 51, **58**; 61-7964 **52**, 53, **53**, 54; 61-7967 60, **61**;61-7972 18, **D31(30)**, **45**, 50, 53; 61-7976 40, **41**, 43, 47; 61-7978 17, **23**, 40; 61-7979 43, **47**; 61-7980 **C21(20)**, **(23)**, **D31(30)**, 42, 44, 54, 55; SR-71B 39, **40**; 61-7956 **B15(14)**, **D31(30)**; 61-7957 14, **14**; SR-71C: 60-6934 **16**
losses and accidents **12**, 12–18, **13**, **B(14)**, **14**, **17**, 44

Mach speeds 5, 9, **10**, 12, **12**, **13**, **17**, **20**, **23**, 24, 25, 26, 27, **27**, 29, 47, **E(48)**
maneuvers 13, 16
McNamara, Robert **6**, 9
Middle East unrest 43–45, 50, 54–55
missile system 5–6
MPC (Mobile Processing Center) at Mildenhall 51–52
MRS (Mission Recorder System) 30
museums **A(10)**, 19, **D(30)**, 59

NASA aeronautical experiments **A(10)**, **19**, 19–20, **C21(20)**
navigation systems 5–6, 14, 30, **30**
nicknames 40
Nixon, Richard 44, 45
North Korea operations 46–48, **E49(48)**

OBC (Optical Bar Camera) **19**, 32, 33, **54**
oil supply 25, 44, 50
O'Malley, Gen. Jerry 56–58
operational control of reconnaissance programs 39–40
Operations: Black Shield (May 1967–May 1968) 9–10, 40, **41**; Desert Storm (January–February 1991 59; El Dorado Canyon (April 1986) **54**, 55
organizational restructuring 55–56
Oxcart program, the 9–10, 34, 39, **41**

PARPRO 51–52, 62
PHOTINT (Photo Intelligence) 46, 51
photo intelligence of Soviet bases 50–51, 52, 54
Pratt & Whitney J58 engines **8**, 22, 23, 24–25, **26**, 27
presidential approval 7–8
pressure suit **37**, 37–38
production 7, **23**
proposed reconnaissance design versions 6–7

prototypes: B-70 Valkyrie bomber 6; SR-71A **7**, **A11(10)**, 13; YF-12 interceptor 4, 5, **6**, 19

radar systems 5–6, 10, **18**, 22, **30**, 32, 35–37, 40, 46, **51**
RADINT (Radar Intelligence) 10, 46
radio call signs 8, **9**, **13**, **40**, **52**
RAF Mildenhall **18**, 33, 43, **47**, 50–51, 53, 54, **58**
RAM (Radar Absorbent Material) 23, **23**
RB-12/RS-12 design version 5, 6, 7
RCS (radar cross section) 4, **5**, 22, 23, **23**
reactivation of SR-71 aircraft 59–60
Reagan, Ronald 47, 48, 55
reconnaissance 4, 7–8, 9–10, 32–36, **33**, **34**, **35**, **36**, 39, 40–44, 42, **43**, **44**, 45, 46–48, 50–52, 53–54
records **45**, 45–46, **46**, 50
refinements in design 7, 14, **19**
refusal of North Korea to allow inspection of nuclear sites 59
replacement of analog systems 27–28
retiring of the SR-71 58–59, **59**, 61
RSO (Reconnaissance Systems Operator) 22, 30, 32, 34

SAM (surface-to-air) missile threats 35–36, 42, **(43)**, 47, **E49(48)**, 50, 52
SAS (Stability Augmentation System) 29–30
satellite capabilities 62
Senate Committees 58, 59, 61
Senior Crown (codename) program 4, 39, **44**, 55–56, 58, **58**, 59, **59**, 62
sensors 32–33, **33**, **36**
serial number changes **18**, 19–20
SIGINT receivers 34–35
SKN-2417 (Singer-Kearfott Inertial Navigation System) 30
Soviet-backed attack on Israel 43–45
Soviet naval exercise details 41–42
speed performance 8, 20, 24, 25, 26–27, **27**, 29, 30, **D30**, 37, 42, 45, **45**, 46, **46**, 50
SRC (Strategic Reconnaissance Center) 39
SSMs (surface-to-surface missiles) 9
stealth technology 4, 62
survival systems **37**, 37–38

tail art **D31(30)**, 61
TEB (Triethylborane) 24, **26**
TEOCs (Technical Objective Cameras) 32, 34, 40
testing 8–9, **12**, 12–16, **13**, 18, **19**, 19–20, **C21(20)**
thermal heating 41
thermodynamic heating 22, **22**, 23
tires 16, **17**, **28**
titanium as construction material 22, **22**
training 38–39, **40**, 51, 52, 62
tricycle undercarriage **28**
trim drag 12, 22
TROC (Terrain Objective Camera) **42**, **43**

"unstarted" engine due to pressure loss 27
USAF: AFLC (Air Force Logistics Command) 27; Det 51/6 18; Air Staff Operations Division XOORZ/XXORS 56, 58; SAC (Strategic Air Command) 6, 39, 46, 50, 51, 56; 9th (4200th) SRW (Strategic Reconnaissance Wing) 13, 39–40; Det 1 (OL-8/OLRK/OLRA) 40, 41, 46, 48; Det 4 33, 53, 54–55, 58; 98th SW/306th SW 51; Det 1 50

V/H (Velocity/Height ratio) system 32, 33
V/R (Velocity/Radial) distance 32
viability of bombers as delivery platform for nuclear weapons 6

wing structure 22–23

yaw conditions 27, 28, 29, 34
Yemeni war threat 53
Yom Kippur War, the 43–45, 50